Geothermal Power

Other books in the Fueling the Future series:

Geothermal Power

Lorraine Savage, *Book Editor*

Christine Nasso, *Publisher*
Elizabeth Des Chenes, *Managing Editor*

GREENHAVEN PRESS
An imprint of Thomson Gale, a part of The Thomson Corporation

THOMSON

GALE

Detroit • New York • San Francisco • New Haven, Conn. • Waterville, Maine • London

For more information, contact
Greenhaven Press
27500 Drake Rd.
Farmington Hills, MI 48331-3535
Or you can visit our Internet site at http://www.gale.com

LIBRARY OF CONGRESS CATALOGING-IN-PUBLICATION DATA

Geothermal power / Lorraine Savage, book editor.
    p. cm. — (Fueling the future)
Includes bibliographical references and index.
ISBN-13: 978-0-7377-3579-6 (hardcover : alk. paper)
ISBN-10: 0-7377-3579-1 (hardcover : alk. paper)
  1. Geothermal engineering—Juvenile literature. 2. Geothermal resources—Juvenile literature. I. Savage, Lorraine.
TJ280.7.G446 2006
621.44—dc22
                                      2006025783

Printed in the United States of America

Contents

Foreword

The wind farm at Altamont Pass in Northern California epitomizes many people's idea of wind power: Hundreds of towering white turbines generate electricity to power homes, factories, and businesses. The spinning turbine blades call up visions of a brighter future in which clean, renewable energy sources replace dwindling and polluting fossil fuels. The blades also kill over a thousand birds of prey each year. Every energy source, it seems, has its price.

The bird deaths at Altamont Pass make clear an unfortunate fact about all energy sources, including renewables: They have downsides. People want clean, abundant energy to power their modern lifestyles, but few want to pay the costs associated with energy production and use. Oil, coal, and natural gas contain high amounts of energy, but using them produces pollution. Commercial solar energy facilities require hundreds of acres of land and thus must be located in rural areas. Expensive and ugly transmission lines must then be run from the solar plants to the cities that need power. Producing hydrogen for fuel involves the use of dirty fossil fuels, tapping geothermal energy depletes ground water, and growing biomass for fuel ties up land that could be used to grow food. Hydroelectric power has become increasingly unpopular because dams flood vital habitats and kill wildlife and plants. Perhaps most controversial, nuclear power plants produce highly dangerous radioactive waste. People's reluctance to pay these environmental costs can be seen in the results of a 2006 Center for Economic and Civic Opinion poll. When asked how much they would support a power plant in their neighborhood, 66 percent of respondents said they would oppose it.

Many scientists warn that fossil fuel use creates emissions that threaten human health and cause global warming. Moreover, numerous scientists claim that fossil fuels are running out. As a result of these concerns, many nations have begun to revisit the energy sources that first powered human enterprises. In his 2006 State of the Union speech, U.S. President George W. Bush announced that since 2001 the United States has spent "$10 billion to develop cleaner, cheaper, and more reliable alternative energy sources," such as biomass and wind power. Despite Bush's positive rhetoric, many critics contend that the renewable energy sources he refers to are still as inefficient as they ever were and cannot possibly power modern economies. As Jerry Taylor and Peter Van Doren of the Cato Institute note, "The market share for non-hydro renewable energy . . . has languished between 1 and 3 percent for decades." Controversies such as this have been a constant throughout the history of humanity's search for the perfect energy source.

Greenhaven Press's Fueling the Future series explores this history. Each volume in the series traces the development of one energy source, and investigates the controversies surrounding its environmental impact and its potential to power humanity's future. The anthologies provide a variety of selections written by scientists, environmental activists, industry leaders, and government experts. Volumes also contain useful research tools, including an introductory essay providing important context, and an annotated table of contents that enables students to locate selections of interest easily. In addition, each volume includes an index, chronology, bibliography, glossary, and a Facts About section, which lists useful information about each energy source. Other features include numerous charts, graphs, and cartoons, which offer additional avenues for learning important information about the topic.

Fueling the Future volumes provide students with important resources for learning about the energy sources upon which human societies depend. Although it is easy to take energy for granted in developed nations, this series emphasizes how energy sources are also problematic. The U.S. Energy Information Administration calls energy "essential to life." Whether scientists will be able to develop the energy sources necessary to sustain modern life is the vital question explored in Greenhaven Press's Fueling the Future series.

Introduction

The fortunes of geothermal energy—energy produced naturally within Earth from decaying radioactive particles in rock—have largely depended upon the fortunes of another energy source: oil. When oil prices rise, interest in geothermal energy increases. Conversely, when oil prices fall, so does investment in geothermal research. Erratic oil prices have largely been the result of an unstable Middle East, which is one of the world's biggest oil suppliers. During wars or other conflicts in the region, oil supplies constrict, resulting in higher prices. During these times of unrest, geothermal development in the United States has gotten the most attention. That interest has proven to be short-lived, however. When crises in the Middle East are resolved, oil prices drop, and investment in geothermal energy declines.

These trends are easy to understand. People want to pay the least they can for the products they consume, whether it be athletic shoes or energy. If one store sells a pair of athletic shoes for eighty dollars while another sells the equivalent pair for ninety-five dollars, most consumers will shop at the store selling the shoes for less money. The same principle works for energy. One of the reasons that the United States uses so much oil is that it has long been a cheap source of energy compared to other sources. As long as oil can be purchased inexpensively from oil-rich nations, there is no pressure to develop other sources of energy. Two trends have made this reliance on foreign oil seem increasingly unwise, however. The first development is rising unpredictability in oil prices, and the second is increased environmental concerns.

Unpredictable Oil Prices

After a long period of stability, oil prices spiked in 1973, when conflict in the Middle East intensified. America sided with Israel in the Arab-Israeli conflict called the Yom Kippur War of

1973, which earned the United States the ire of Arab nations. In retaliation, the Arab members of the Organization of Petroleum Exporting Countries (OPEC) imposed an oil embargo against the United States and its allies, Europe and Japan. The result was an increase in oil prices from three dollars a barrel to twelve dollars. Rising oil prices caused U.S. inflation to peak, resulting in a recession. Oil prices increased again in the late 1970s and early 1980s as a result of the Iranian Revolution, the Iran hostage crisis, and Iraq's invasion of Kuwait. During this time, the price of oil rose from fifteen dollars a barrel to peak at thirty-nine dollars a barrel in 1980.

Not surprisingly, this sudden rise in oil prices encouraged the United States to investigate other energy sources. Nuclear, solar, wind, water, and geothermal energy development all received increased federal funding during this era. Before the oil

Off the Wagon

Jeff Danziger. Reproduced by permission.

crisis, only $2.5 million had been budgeted for geothermal research and production. By 1976 federal funding for geothermal research reached $91 million, nearly forty times more than the funding level in 1973.

Other developments led to increased investment in geothermal energy. In direct response to the oil embargo, Congress passed the Geothermal Energy Research, Development, and Demonstration Act in 1974 to aid the evaluation of geothermal resources. Also, the Energy Research and Development Administration was created to increase federal research into alternative forms of energy. As the oil crisis continued, Congress passed the 1978 U.S. Public Utility Regulatory Policies Act, which encouraged energy efficiency and required power plants to use some renewable energy, such as geothermal power.

Despite Interest in Geothermal Energy, Its Fortunes Decline

Despite its potential, investment in geothermal energy still lagged far behind investment in oil. For example, from 1972 to 1977, roughly 150 new geothermal wells were drilled compared to about 140,000 oil wells. Clearly, while the United States was eager to wean itself off of Middle East oil, it chose to put more of its investment into increased domestic oil drilling than in developing alternative energy sources.

While many experts agreed that Earth's free heat source was worth exploiting, they had doubts about whether that energy could be obtained and distributed affordably. In 1977 energy researcher Daniel S. Halacy Jr. summed up these concerns: "Although it is well agreed that the heat energy in the outer six miles of Earth's crust may be 2,000 times greater than that of all the world's coal, making use of it is something else again. Best guesses are that we may never recover more than a fraction of one percent of that tantalizing total of geothermal heat." In 1979 the National Academy of Science lamented that geothermal "provides very little useful energy, and the technical and economic barriers it faces make it unlikely to become one of the nation's main energy sources before the end of this century, if ever."

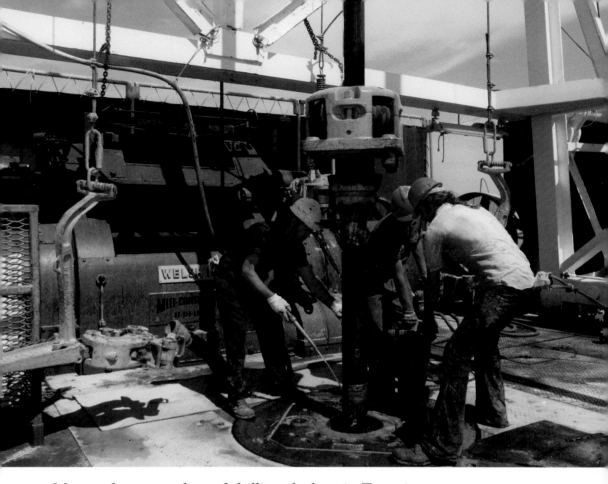

Men work on a geothermal drilling platform in Texas in 1978. Interest in geothermal energy grew during the oil shortages of the 1970s.

The basic problem with geothermal energy is that it is expensive. The risks associated with geothermal resource exploration (what if no resources are found?), the high level of investment needed to develop a geothermal resource if discovered, and the slow return on that investment act as deterrents to geothermal development. Moreover, although geothermal is considered a renewable energy source, extracting hot water and steam from beneath the earth's crust often results in the well drying up. Some dried-up reservoirs need to lie dormant for years before they can replenish themselves and be used again to obtain geothermal energy.

These downsides to geothermal energy have helped prevent it from becoming one of America's major energy sources. Perhaps more important, the price of oil has simply not gotten high enough to encourage a shift to geothermal energy. People do not want to pay more for geothermal when they can pay much less for oil. Evidence for this can be seen in the mid-1980s. As conflicts in the Middle East subsided, OPEC began reducing the price of oil, which returned to a low of fifteen dollars a barrel in 1986. The drop in oil prices extinguished much of the interest in geothermal energy. The U.S. Department of Energy's funding for geothermal energy research and development declined, reaching a low of $15 million in 1990.

New Developments Spark Renewed Interest in Geothermal Energy

In the face of lapsing interest in geothermal energy, representatives from the geothermal industry appeared before Congress to promote the energy source as an environmentally responsible energy technology. Partly as a result of their efforts, Congress passed the Energy Policy Act of 1992, which required utility companies to develop renewable fuels and reduce greenhouse gases. During this time, increasing numbers of scientists warned that the burning of fossil fuels emitted greenhouse gases that increased global warming. According to these scientists, the warming was raising sea levels, causing polar ice to melt, and producing severe weather. Geothermal energy production, since it emits no greenhouse gases, was touted as a way to reduce global warming.

In lauding the environmental benefits of geothermal energy, proponents could not neglect economics. Advocates claimed that geothermal energy development contributed significantly to local economies by creating jobs and raising revenue. Supporters claimed that businesses could use geothermal power to warm greenhouses and heat water for aquaculture, and farmers could grow plants in colder climates. Geothermal power could even help public schools and universities. By installing geothermal heating systems, their heating bills could be lowered. Advocates also pointed out that individuals could lower their heating bills by installing geothermal heat pumps in their homes. The heat pumps tap Earth's natural heat below the ground and pipe it into a home to warm it.

Many energy experts think that recent political events will renew interest in geothermal energy. The September 11, 2001, terrorist attacks, perpetrated by Middle Eastern terrorists, made clear how tenuous are the relationships between the United States and the Arab nations that supply a large portion of the world's oil. Many people believe that the controversial 2003 Iraq War was fought to secure access to a significant part of that oil supply. Sharply rising oil prices in 2005 and 2006 brought back memories of the 1973 oil embargo: In April 2006 the price of oil set record highs for three consecutive days, peaking at seventy-five dollars a barrel. While these events have spurred

Plumes of steam billow out of a geothermal power plant in Iceland. Renewed interest in geothermal and other renewable energies is tied to unstable world politics.

investment into energy alternatives generally, the interest in geothermal energy is mixed. The U.S. Department of Energy's preliminary budget for 2007 calls for elimination of the Geothermal Technologies Program, with funding instead allocated to hydrogen and biomass technologies. At the same time, the Energy Policy Act of 2005 raises funding for the program to $32.5 million for 2007.

The Future of Geothermal Energy Is Uncertain

Fossil fuels such as oil are finite. While controversy exists about how long fossil fuel supplies will last, it is clear that more countries are unwilling to build their futures completely on oil, coal, and natural gas. As the United States increases investment in energy alternatives, geothermal must compete for funding with other sources such as biomass and hydrogen. To be sure, with Earth's own enormous heat ready to be tapped, scientists will continue to work on ways to extract that energy more economically. Whether they succeed or not will depend on the success of other energy alternatives, the level of concern over global warming, and, of course, the ever-fluctuating price of oil.

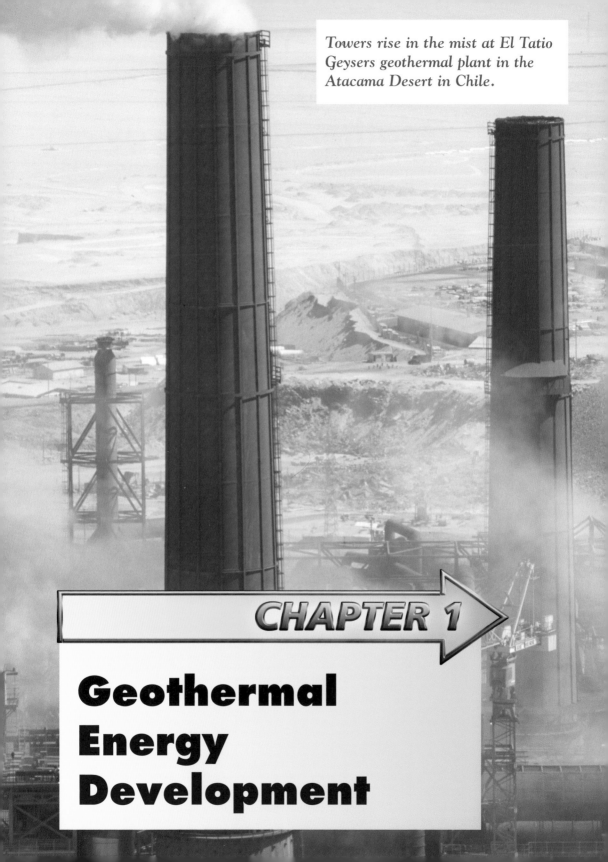

Towers rise in the mist at El Tatio Geysers geothermal plant in the Atacama Desert in Chile.

CHAPTER 1

Geothermal Energy Development

The History of Geothermal Energy

Daniel S. Halacy Jr.

Daniel S. Halacy Jr. explains in the following selection that geothermal energy is heat that is generated from the decay of nuclear materials deep underground. He notes that lava from volcanoes, geysers, and hot springs are all signs of geothermal activity. Thousands of years ago, according to Halacy, the Greeks, Romans, Japanese, and Native Americans used hot springs for bathing and washing. More than a hundred years ago Europeans began drilling to tap into geothermal heat directly. Today, facilities in Larderello, Italy, are reclaiming useful chemicals, such as boric acid, from hot springs. Moreover, Iceland has a thriving geothermal industry that heats businesses, private homes, and industry. In the United States, Halacy says, geothermal drilling initially began at The Geysers in California in 1922 to heat a hot springs resort, but it has now grown into an expansive enterprise. Halacy has worked in the aircraft and electronics industries, taught at Phoenix College, and was an Arizona state senator. He is the author of dozens of books on alternative energy, weather, genetics, and world hunger.

It has often been suggested that Dante [Alighieri's] vivid vision of hell [in his book *Inferno*] was conjured up by visits to the strange Larderello [Italy] area, where sulfurous fumaroles, mudpots, craters, and boiling wells splotched the land. This outpouring of geothermal energy was indeed triggered by molten rocks in the bowels of Earth.

The hellish connotation of geothermal wells has been softened since Dante's time, and most of us are more likely to think of the geyser Old Faithful at Yellowstone Park. Less known is The Geysers, a geothermal site in northern California, subterranean steam producing some 400 megawatts of electricity for the power lines of the Pacific Gas & Electric Company, more than half the needs of San Francisco. Here is the reason for the keen interest suddenly focused on this long-known but little-used alternative. . . .

Geothermal's Past

The most obvious indicators of geothermal activity are the hot springs that flow abundantly on Earth's surface. These steamy hints of what lies deeper have been known for ages and have been put to good use for the last two thousand or more years. Hot water is basically useful for bathing and washing clothes. In time, people came to attribute medicinal value to hot springs or

Thousands of years ago, Romans used these geothermal springs in Bath, England, the only natural hot springs in the country.

The Source of Geothermal Energy

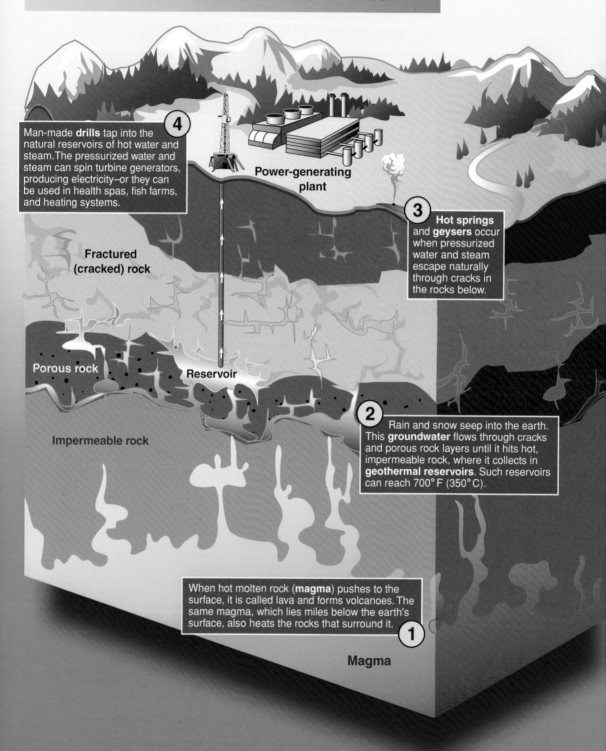

Man-made **drills** tap into the natural reservoirs of hot water and steam. The pressurized water and steam can spin turbine generators, producing electricity—or they can be used in health spas, fish farms, and heating systems.

④

Power-generating plant

③ Hot springs and **geysers** occur when pressurized water and steam escape naturally through cracks in the rocks below.

Fractured (cracked) rock

Porous rock

Reservoir

② Rain and snow seep into the earth. This **groundwater** flows through cracks and porous rock layers until it hits hot, impermeable rock, where it collects in **geothermal reservoirs**. Such reservoirs can reach 700° F (350° C).

Impermeable rock

When hot molten rock (**magma**) pushes to the surface, it is called lava and forms volcanoes. The same magma, which lies miles below the earth's surface, also heats the rocks that surround it.

①

Magma

Sources: U.S. Department of Energy (www.eere.energy.gov) and Geothermal Education Office (http://geothermal.marin.org).

"spas." The ancient Greeks, Romans, and Babylonians, and the Japanese are among those who knew and used hot springs for curative as well as recreational purposes.

The Romans developed hot springs throughout their empire, as far north as Bath, England. Later the Hapsburgs established the famous Marienbad and Karlsbad spas in Czechoslovakia. More than a century ago Hungarians went nature one better and *drilled* a well to reach geothermal water. "Taking the waters" has long been a way of life, and President Franklin D. Roosevelt helped popularize Warm Springs, Georgia, to whose mineral pools he went often to bathe.

Dante may have equated Larderello's vaporous springs with hell, but the Icelandic concept of hell is a frozen horror of ice and snow. To the Icelanders the phenomenon of boiling hot water from the cold ground must have seemed instead a miracle from heaven. All around the world human beings have used geothermal waters for a variety of purposes, including bathing, washing, agriculture, cooking, and for the recovery of byprod-ucts like boric acid, sulfur, and other chemicals. At first, geo-thermal energy was roughly the reverse of lake ice cut into blocks and packed in sawdust for its cooling magic in summer. But in 1904 a new age of geothermal energy began when engi-neers tapped the steam from Larderello to run a 3/4-horsepower generator and light five light bulbs. It was a tiny effort, but it proved a principle: heat from deep within the Earth could run an electric power plant. Today the output from Larderello has grown from five light bulbs to 400 megawatts of power, enough to fill the electric needs of about half a million people.

The Waters Under the Earth

It has been pointed out that the Earth was born hot and still has not cooled down. While the crust we live on is quite comfort-able most of the time, the temperature increases as one bores down through that crust. As miners know, the increase is some-thing like 100 degrees F. per mile. At the base of the "continen-tal crust," the temperature may be as high as 1,800 degrees F., and at Earth's center something like 8,000 degrees F. Should we ever succeed in running a pipe (of material able to withstand such temperature) into that hot furnace, we could draw on a fantastic reservoir of heat energy. The fact that we now dig no deeper than six miles or so lessens the geothermal potential, but even so it is remarkable.

Experts believe that most geothermal heat is caused by the decay of nuclear materials deep in the Earth, with some heat coming from the friction of rock movement, tidal forces, and perhaps other sources. Whatever the causes, it is a fact that beneath the crust lie great quantities of molten rock, or "magma." Occasionally this magma breaks through to push up as lava in volcanoes. Not as spectacularly, but more regularly, geothermal heat from magma reaches the surface as hot water. In a few places it does this in a spectacular manner as highly pressurized hot water is vented to the air and turns to steam.

Two ingredients are necessary for the production of geothermal wells: magma, or hot rocks, and a source of water. There is discussion whether this is surface water, or new water produced from elemental materials. Whatever the source, water heated by magma in certain areas is available for a variety of tasks, ranging from fish farming to generating electricity.

Forms of Geothermal Energy

Geothermal energy is available in four forms: dry steam, wet steam, hot rocks, and geopressured deposits. Dry steam is ideal for producing power, since it causes no corrosion of turbines or associated equipment and is the most potent heat source because of its very high temperature. Wet steam is also a useful source but must be cleaned up so that it won't harm generating equipment. Hot rocks are tantalizing geothermal sources, but water must be introduced artificially to the dry heat source to produce steam or hot water. . . .

Geopressured deposits have been trapped for ages by clay beds and are much hotter than normal underground water. Such deposits occur even in areas where there are no volcanoes, earthquake faulting, or mountain building. In the United States the largest area of geopressured water is along the Gulf Coast. There are two unusual things about such geothermal deposits. First, the water is very low in salinity, since it has been effectively filtered by clay and perhaps by shale as well. Second, the water may also contain appreciable amounts of natural gas— up to a cubic meter of gas per barrel of water. Thus there is a double reason for seeking such resources. . . .

Putting Geothermal Energy to Work

Primitive use of geothermal springs is many centuries old, as we have noted. A century and a half ago some people were beginning to exploit this source in other ways. Wells were drilled for hot water, and chemicals were reclaimed from hot springs, notably at Larderello where a thriving boric acid industry sprang up. By 1900 hot-water drilling was common in Italy, Hungary, Germany, and Iceland. Budapest accomplished geothermal home heating in the 1930s, and by the early 1940s Reykjavik, Iceland, was using geothermal hot water for home heating and industry. New Zealand, notably at Rotorua, was doing the same thing. Japanese farmers heated greenhouses with hot springs shortly after the turn of the century.

Russia too has heated homes for a long time with geothermal springs. More recently Russia's engineers have gotten into power generation. So have engineers in Mexico and El Salvador. Other interested nations include Ethiopia, Kenya, the Philippines, Indonesia, Chile, Turkey, Katanga, Zaire, Nicaragua, and France.

Geothermal Development in the United States

With its more than one thousand geothermal springs, the United States has known for a long time about geothermal

In 1980, a scientist tests geothermal fluid from a well in Yellowstone National Park, an area of intense geothermal activity.

energy. Yellowstone, protected by law against exploitation along with geothermal fields at Katmai and Lassen National Parks, has long demonstrated the tremendous power pushing its way through Earth's crust. Test drilling was done at Yellowstone in the 1920s and 1930s; in 1967 and 1969 more sophisticated prospecting turned up 240-degree C. water at a depth of only 300 meters.

California, site of the great gold rush, was also a leader in geothermal exploitation. In the 1920s pioneers bored wells at Niland, near the Salton Sea. There was plenty of low-temperature steam, but the project was abandoned because of a lack of a market for this commodity. At the northeast end of the Niland field shallow wells produced carbon dioxide, however, and this gas did have commercial value. From the early 1930s through the mid-1950s some sixty-five wells were drilled, with about 100 million cubic meters of carbon dioxide produced to make dry ice for refrigerator cars.

While the Niland pioneers were working the southern part of the state, prospectors northeast of San Francisco hit steam in the area logically named The Geysers. The place was discovered by explorer William Bell Elliott in 1847 when he blundered into a canyon where steam poured from fissures along a quarter-mile length. . . .

In 1922 drillers attempted to harness The Geysers for electric power but succeeded only in lighting the hot springs resort which had sprung up. Steam corroded the engines and plumbing, and there was plenty of hydroelectric power in the neighborhood. In short, the United States wasn't ready for geothermal power, and would not be for several decades. For years the extent of geothermal applications was for agriculture, fish farming, bathing, and house heating as at Boise, Idaho, and Klamath Falls, Oregon, and use of hot water in explosives manufacture at Steamboat Springs, Nevada. But the potential was too great, and in 1956 a second wave of engineers tackled The Geysers.

Magma Power Company and Thermal Power Company drilled wells in The Geysers area and began producing dry steam. In 1960 Pacific Gas & Electric contracted with them to buy the steam, and in short order caught up with and surpassed the output of Italy's impressive Larderello geothermal plants.

Uses for Geothermal Power Generation

Television Trust for the Environment

In the following selection Television Trust for the Environment describes geothermal energy as natural heat within Earth. According to the organization, geothermal is a renewable source of energy that can meet a variety of energy needs. High-temperature sources of geothermal energy are used for producing electric power, while low-temperature sources are used for direct heating of buildings and for agricultural applications such as heating greenhouses. Larderello, Italy, has used geothermal energy since 1865. Today, geothermal energy produces heat for 2 million households in Larderello and heats the region's swimming pools, greenhouses, and industrial plants. Television Trust for the Environment is an independent, nonprofit organization that promotes global awareness of the environment.

Many countries around the world exploit geothermal resources to significantly reduce consumption of imported fossil fuels. In the west of Italy there is a long belt of land in the Tuscany region and extending as far south as Campania, near Naples, where very high temperatures, often exceeding 200°C (392°F), are located not far below the surface. Geothermal energy has been used here ever since 1865 when the first pumps propelled with geothermal steam were installed.

Television Trust for the Environment, "Full Steam Ahead, Italy," www.tve.org, September 2002. Reproduced by permission.

Currently the geothermal energy produced in Larderello, in Tuscany, provides around two million households with heating, as well as supplying heat to greenhouses and fish farms, satisfying a great part of the energy needs of the Tuscany region.

In Larderello, the local swimming pool has re-opened after many years of closure and features a brand-new geothermal heating system. New greenhouses have been built in the Radicondoli area, and an industrial plant for the processing of dairy by-products has been set up in Carboli, in the southernmost part of Larderello.

In 1950 an engineer checks the valves at the power plant in Larderello, Italy. The area has a long history of geothermal energy use.

Types of Geothermal Plants

Geothermal power plants convert hot water and steam to electricity. The type of plant depends on the temperature of the water as it comes from the geothermal reservoir.

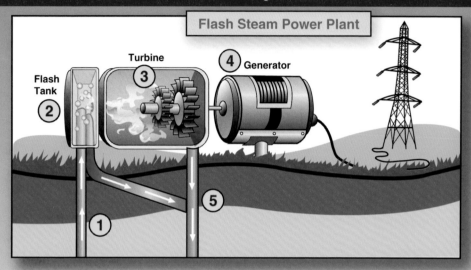

Flash Steam Power Plant

Turbine

③

④ Generator

Flash Tank

②

①

⑤

The most common type of geothermal power plant is a flash steam power plant, which uses very hot water (over 360°F/182°C) under high pressure. As superheated water rushes to the surface (1), the water pressure suddenly decreases, causing the water to boil and turn (or "flash") into steam (2). The steam is used to power a turbine (3) that generates electricity (4). Leftover water is pumped back into the reservoir (5) for reuse.

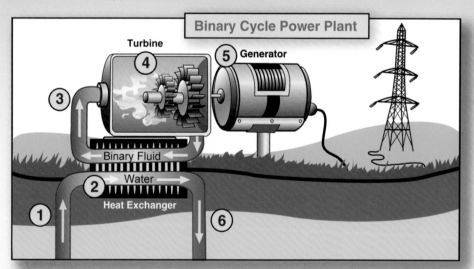

Binary Cycle Power Plant

Turbine

④

⑤ Generator

③

Binary Fluid

Water

② Heat Exchanger

①

⑥

Binary cycle power plants use water at medium-hot temperatures (212°–360°F, or 100°–150°C). The hot water is piped from a production well (1) into a heat exchanger (2) together with another fluid having a lower boiling point. The second (or "binary") fluid boils and vaporizes (3). The vapor spins a turbine (4) to generate electricity (5). The leftover water and condensed steam are injected back into the earth (6) to be reheated and reused. The binary fluid remains in the system and is also reused.

Sources: U.S. Department of Energy (www.doe.gov, www.eere.energy.gov) and the National Renewable Energy Laboratory (www.nrel.gov).

The long-term sustainability of geothermal production has been demonstrated by continuous electrical power generation in Larderello since 1913, when a 250 kW [kilowatt] power station supplied power to the Italian railway system. Italy is now the fourth largest producer of geothermal energy in the world. Approximately 2 per cent of its population is provided with energy from geothermal sources.

High and Low Temperature Sources of Geothermal Energy

Heat exchangers are used to extract the heat from the hot geothermal fluid. As this fluid often contains chemicals, it cannot be used directly in drying processes or where clean steam or hot water is necessary. Heat exchangers transfer the heat either to clean water or, in the case of drying processes, to air.

High temperature sources are almost always used for power production. Individual geothermal power plants can be as small as 100 kilowatts (kW) or as large as 100 MW [megawatts], depending on the energy resource and power demand. The technology is suitable for rural electrification and mini-grid applications in addition to national grid applications.

Most low temperature sources are used for direct heating purposes or agriculture and aquaculture. For such direct use technologies, since geothermal heat is non-transportable (except short distances by pipeline), any applications must generally be sited within 10 km (about six miles) of the resource. Pumps are frequently used to carry the water to the surface.

Low temperature sources can provide useful energy for heating buildings and for agricultural and industrial processes. Such heat can also be available as a by-product of geothermal power generation.

This energy is used for agriculture and aquaculture. In temperate and colder climates, greatly improved plant and fish growth can be achieved by heating soils, greenhouses and fishponds using geothermal heat. It can also be used for medicinal purposes and balneology, the practice of using natural mineral water for the treatment and cure of disease, such as in spa pools.

Uses in Agriculture, Aquaculture, and Industry

Thermal water can be used in open-field agriculture to irrigate and/or heat the soil and also to sterilise soil. Geothermal heat can also be used for crop and timber drying.

A researcher holds a large shrimp from a geothermal pond. Low temperature geothermal energy is ideal for aquaculture.

The main advantages of temperature control in open-field agriculture are:

- the prevention of plant damage from low air temperatures;
- extension of the growing season;
- increased plant growth and production; and
- soil sterilisation that controls pests and diseases.

Greenhouse heating is a common use of geothermal energy. Glass or plastic film is used to trap solar radiation and heat, which provides a controlled environment for plants to grow and increase yields. Many commercially grown vegetables, flowers, house plants and tree seedlings are suitable for greenhouse culture.

Aquaculture is the farming of aquatic organisms including fish, molluscs, crustaceans and aquatic plants. Farming implies some sort of intervention in the rearing process to enhance production, such as regular stocking, feeding, and protection from predators. In geothermal aquaculture the objective is to heat the water to the optimum temperature for fish growth. An emerging aquacultural industry is the cultivation of vegetable species that can be adapted for human and animal foods. Crops adaptable to geothermal enhanced growth include duckweed, numerous algae species and kelp.

Geothermal energy can be cost effective and reliable in industrial applications. Some industries use steam, or superheated water, and starting with warm water obviously reduces the amount of heat required. The largest industrial applications are in pulp, paper and wood processing.

Geothermal heat pumps enable the resources to be used economically. Ground-coupled heat pumps use earth-temperature soil for heating during winter, cooling during summer, and supplying hot water year-round. Water-to-air heat pumps exchange heat with groundwater, surface water or water passed through cooling towers for industrial and commercial uses. . . .

The Future of Geothermal Energy

Thanks to geothermal energy, millions of tonnes of fossil fuels are being saved worldwide and polluting emissions are being greatly reduced. It is one of the few technologies that significantly contributes to reducing greenhouse gas emissions. If geothermal energy continues to be used at the present rate, it is estimated that the available resources could last for five million years.

Current geothermal technologies use only a tiny fraction of total geothermal resources. Several miles beneath Earth's surface is hot, dry rock being heated by the molten magma directly below. Technology is now being developed to drill into this rock, inject cold water down a well, circulate it through the hot, fractured rock, and draw off the heated water from a different well. This has the potential to supply the energy needs of the entire world for centuries to come.

The Advantages and Disadvantages of Geothermal Energy

National Geothermal Collaborative

According to the National Geothermal Collaborative (NGC) in this selection, geothermal energy is a reliable source of power that produces energy 98 percent of the time. The organization also states that geothermal plants produce fewer harmful emissions than do other power plants. However, NGC explains that geothermal energy has several drawbacks. For example, most geothermal resources are located in remote areas, requiring energy companies to run miles of power lines from geothermal sites to the cities that need power. Another problem is that drilling is risky and costly, with only one in five wells dug locating a usable source of geothermal energy. The National Geothermal Collaborative is an organization working to overcome obstacles to geothermal development.

Geothermal energy can play an important part in a state's energy policy. In addition to identifying the benefits of geothermal energy, this brief also identifies some of the main challenges such as transmission constraints and regulatory barriers.

Reliable Power

One of the principal benefits of geothermal power plants is that they provide baseload power. Baseload power plants provide power all or most of the time and contrast with "peaker" plants

National Geothermal Collaborative, "Benefits of Geothermal Energy," National Geothermal Collaborative. Reproduced by permission.

which turn on or off as demand rises, or peaks, throughout the day. Geothermal plants contrast with other renewable energy resources like wind and solar energy that generate power intermittently. Geothermal plants in the United States are available to operate approximately 98 percent of the time. Such high percentages make them compare favorably with fossil fuel and nuclear power plants that operate between 75 and 90 percent of the time depending on the technology and age of the equipment.

Geothermal resources can provide power for many years. The Geysers geothermal field for example, which began commercial production in 1960 in Northern California, had the first domestic geothermal power plant. Nearly half a century later, the 21 power plants operating there generate power for approximately one million households in California. The key to successful long-term sustainable geothermal production lies in efficiently managing the resource. Technological advances—such as water injection, continue to be developed and allow developers to maximize resources and minimize drilling.

Electricity at Stable Prices

Using geothermal resources for power can help protect against volatile electricity prices. For any power plant, the price of the fuel used to generate power influences the price of the electricity produced; if the price of fuel is unpredictable, the price of electricity is unpredictable. Unlike traditional power plants that require fuel purchases, geothermal power plants secure their fuel supply before the plants begin operating. Since the price of geothermal resources will not change, it is possible to know what the price of electricity generated at a geothermal power plant will be over time. The price of electricity from new geothermal power plants ranges from between $0.05 per kWh [per kilowatt-hour] and $0.08 per kWh. Once capital costs for the projects are recovered, the price of power can decrease below $0.05 per kWh. Fossil fuels have traditionally generated power for less, but the price of these fuels can suddenly increase to a level that is more expensive than geothermal electricity. For example, in early 2004 the price of natural gas was nearly three times what it was throughout the 1990s.

This is an aerial view of a geothermal gas turbine at the Larderello power plant in Italy. Geothermal steam turns the turbine for electricity.

Renewable energy resources like geothermal can help states diversify the mix of fuels they rely on for power and protect customers from volatile electricity prices. The fuel costs for a geothermal power plant are not dependent upon volatile markets. In contrast, the price of natural gas is volatile and difficult to predict accurately. . . . In addition, using domestic renewable resources can help states reduce the amount of fuel they import from nearby states or overseas.

Geothermal power plants produce only a small amount of air emissions. Compared to conventional fossil fuel plants, they emit very small amounts of carbon monoxide, particulate matter, sulfur dioxide, carbon dioxide, and typically no nitrogen oxides.

Economic Development Potential

Fifteen states now have some sort of renewable portfolio standard (RPS) that requires power providers to supply a certain amount of their power from renewable resources by a specific year. In many of these states, electricity generated from geothermal resources can count toward meeting the standard.

Using geothermal resources can provide economic development opportunities for states in the form of property taxes, royalty payments and jobs. Geothermal power plants are the largest taxpayer in nearly every county where they exist. The 21 geothermal power plants at the Geysers Geothermal Field in California can generate almost 1,000 MW [megawatts] of electricity and have been an important source of revenue and jobs for Lake and Sonoma counties for many years. These power plants employ approximately 425 people full-time plus an additional full-time equivalent contract work force of 225. In 2003, property tax payments to the two counties totaled more than $11 million.

Another revenue stream flows from royalties that developers pay in exchange for the right to tap resources on federal, state or private lands. These are similar to severance taxes that states charge for extracting fuels or minerals. In 2003, operations at The Geysers generated a total of $6.15 million in federal royalties and $4.1 million in royalties to the State of California. Local county governments share in both the federal and state royalties.

Direct Use Applications

In addition to generating electricity, the heat in geothermal fluids can be used directly for such purposes as growing flowers, raising fish and heating buildings. There are a number of basic types of direct use applications: aquaculture, greenhouses, industrial and agricultural processes, resorts and spas, space and district heating, and cooling. Generally, direct use projects use fluids with temperatures of between 70°F and 300°F. Direct use systems in the United States currently provide approximately 600 thermal megawatts of heat, enough to heat approximately 115,000 average homes. (The power from direct use systems is measured in megawatts of heat as opposed to power plants that measure power in megawatts of electricity.) Some geothermal projects "cascade" geothermal energy by using the same resource for different purposes simultaneously such as heating

A worker walks up the stairs of the cooling tower at The Geysers, the first geothermal power plant built in the United States.

and power. Cascading uses the resource more efficiently and may improve the economics of a project.

Four commercial greenhouses in southern New Mexico, which at times have employed up to 400 people, occupy more than 50 acres and use geothermal heat to grow plants. In 2002, these projects generated nearly $23 million in sales and paid more than $6 million in payroll. A large greenhouse in rural Utah that grows flowers employs between 80 and 120 people at different times throughout the year.

Challenges for Geothermal Energy

There are a variety of technical and regulatory challenges preventing the more widespread use of geothermal power. Leasing and siting processes can take long periods and be fraught with uncertainty. Although the cost of generating power from geothermal resources has decreased by 25 percent during the last two decades, exploration and drilling remain expensive and

Iceland uses greenhouses heated with geothermal energy to grow produce and flowers.

risky. Drilling costs alone can account for as much as one-third to one-half of the total cost of a project and wells typically cost between $1 and $5 million each. Detecting potentially productive geothermal reservoirs is difficult, with only about one in every five exploratory wells drilled confirming a valuable resource. The rate of success increases significantly once the resource has been found. Because some of the best geothermal resources are located in remote areas, tapping them may require an expansion of the power transmission system, which can also be expensive. Finally, power plants and direct use systems must be located near geothermal resources because it is not economic to transport hot water or steam over long distances.

Geothermal Energy Development Expands Globally

U.S. Newswire

According to U.S. Newswire in this selection, geothermal energy is now produced in twenty-four countries. Established geothermal producers—such as France, Russia, and Kenya—have tripled their production since 2000, while Austria, Germany, and Papua New Guinea have just lately begun exploiting this energy source. While the United States is still the world's largest producer of geothermal electricity, other nations such as the Philippines and Indonesia are catching up. U.S. Newswire is a news release wire service.

Geothermal energy is now produced in 24 countries and on all continents except Antarctica, according to a new study by Ruggero Bertani of ENEL [Italy's largest power company], presented at the World Geothermal Congress in Turkey. In 2003, geothermal resource supplied 57,000 Gigawatt-hours of electricity, an increase of 15 percent from 2000 and 50 percent from 1995, Bertani reported.

Since 2000, geothermal generation has tripled in France, Russia, and Kenya, and three new countries—Austria, Germany, and Papua New Guinea—have been added to the list of those producing power. "Geothermal energy is today meeting the total electricity needs of some 60 million people worldwide—roughly the population of the United Kingdom," noted

U.S. Newswire, "Geothermal Power Expands to 24 Countries, Meets the Needs of 60 Million People," *U.S. Newswire*, May 16, 2005. Reproduced by permission.

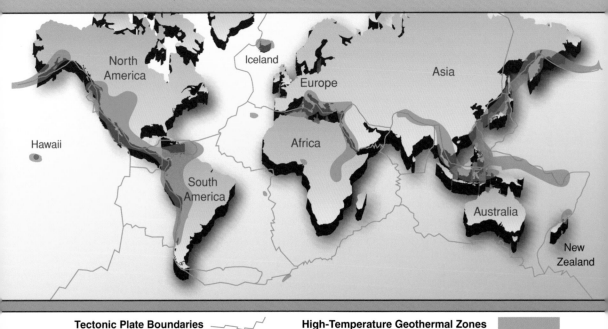

Geothermal Hot Zones Around the World

The earth's crust is composed of tectonic plates, sections of the crust that move constantly, but very slowly, in relation to each other. Volcanoes, earthquakes, and the hottest geothermal resources are all found near tectonic plate boundaries, where magma and hot water are closer to the earth's surface.

Iceland
North America
Europe
Asia
Hawaii
Africa
South America
Australia
New Zealand

Tectonic Plate Boundaries   High-Temperature Geothermal Zones

Source: Energy & Geoscience Institute, University of Utah (www.egi.utah.edu), 2001.

Karl Gawell, Executive Director of GEA [the Geothermal Energy Association], the US industry's trade group. "Countries as diverse as the Philippines, Iceland, and El Salvador generate an average of 25 percent of their electricity from geothermal sources, and geothermal serves 30 percent of Tibet's energy needs," he added.

America Is Losing the Lead

The United States continues to produce more geothermal electricity than any other country, comprising some 32 percent of the world total. But, according to GEA, the US lead in geothermal power production and technology are both being seriously challenged. "Several countries are moving aggressively ahead with new development, particularly the Philippines and Indonesia, and while US research budgets are being cut, other countries are investing more in new technology," Gawell noted. For example, new hot dry rock technology is expected to produce hundreds of megawatts in Australia this year [2005]. This technology could allow geothermal power production virtually anywhere in the world.

Yet, the U.S. geothermal power industry appears to be on a rebound. State renewable policies and federal tax incentives are spurring a wave of new investment. GEA reports that projects are being planned in several states including Alaska, Arizona, California, Hawaii, Idaho, Nevada, New Mexico, and Oregon. "We have just begun to tap the tens of thousands of megawatts of geothermal resources available," Gawell said. "It's just a question of the right economic incentives and continued advances in technology." . . .

Countries producing geothermal power in 2003 were: Australia, Austria, China, Costa Rica, El Salvador, Ethiopia, France (Guadeloupe), Germany, Guatemala, Iceland, Indonesia, Italy, Japan, Kenya, Mexico, New Zealand, Nicaragua, Papua New Guinea, Philippines, Portugal (Azores), Russia, Thailand, Turkey, and the United States.

Geothermal Energy Benefits the Environment

Energy Efficiency and Renewable Energy Office

The U.S. Department of Energy's Energy Efficiency and Renewable Energy Office [EERE] explains in this selection that geothermal power plants help protect air and water quality and have minimal impact on the land. Geothermal production emits very little carbon dioxide, a greenhouse gas, compared to coal and natural gas production. Geothermal energy production does generate some solid byproducts, the EERE concedes, but these often contain valuable minerals that can be recovered for industrial uses. EERE's Geothermal Technologies Program works in partnership with U.S. industries to establish geothermal energy as an economically competitive contributor to the U.S. energy supply.

Geothermal power plants operating in the United States have to meet many federal, state, and local environmental standards and regulations, such as the Clean Air Act.

When local communities use geothermal power plants, they can easily:

- Meet clean air standards
- Minimize solid waste and recover/recycle minerals
- Meet water quality and conservation standards
- Minimize land use and impact.

The Energy Efficiency and Renewable Energy Office, "Environmental Impacts and Benefits of Geothermal Power Plants," www.eere.energy.gov. December 1, 2004. Reproduced by permission.

Harmful Gases Emitted by Power Plants

Carbon Dioxide Emissions

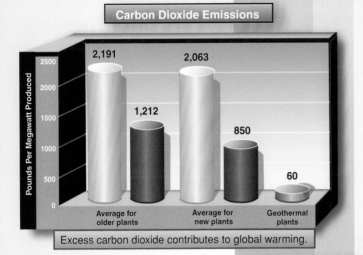

Pounds Per Megawatt Produced

- 2,191 — Average for older plants (Coal)
- 1,212 — Average for older plants (Natural Gas)
- 2,063 — Average for new plants (Coal)
- 850 — Average for new plants (Natural Gas)
- 60 — Geothermal plants

Average for older plants | Average for new plants | Geothermal plants

Excess carbon dioxide contributes to global warming.

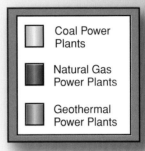

- Coal Power Plants
- Natural Gas Power Plants
- Geothermal Power Plants

Sulfur Dioxide Emissions

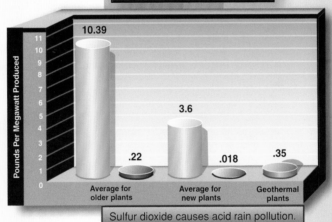

Pounds Per Megawatt Produced

- 10.39 — Average for older plants
- .22
- 3.6 — Average for new plants
- .018
- .35 — Geothermal plants

Average for older plants | Average for new plants | Geothermal plants

Sulfur dioxide causes acid rain pollution.

Nitrogen Oxide Emissions

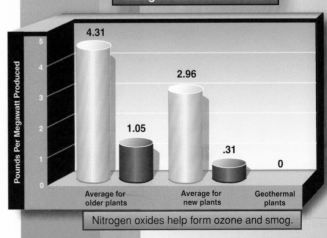

Pounds Per Megawatt Produced

- 4.31 — Average for older plants
- 1.05
- 2.96 — Average for new plants
- .31
- 0 — Geothermal plants

Average for older plants | Average for new plants | Geothermal plants

Nitrogen oxides help form ozone and smog.

Sources: Platts Research and Consulting/
Environmental Protection Agency (coal and
gas data), 2003; U.S. Department of Energy
(geothermal data), 2000.

Meeting Clean Air Standards

Geothermal power plants can meet the most stringent clean air standards. They emit little carbon dioxide, very low amounts of sulfur dioxide, and no nitrogen oxides. . . .

To put this in perspective, electricity produced from U.S. geothermal resources, compared to conventional coal-fired plants, annually offsets the emission of:

- 4.1 million tons of carbon dioxide
- 80,000 tons of nitrogen oxides
- 110,000 tons of particulate matter.

The small quantities of gases emitted from geothermal power plants aren't created during power production because there's no combustion. These gases are natural, minor constituents of all geothermal reservoirs. They eventually would vent to the

A worker inspects a turbine generator inside the Calpine geothermal power plant near Sonoma in northern California.

atmosphere without geothermal power development, although at much slower rates. Dry steam and flash steam power plants emit mostly water vapor. Binary-cycle power plants emit virtually no gases because they operate using a closed-loop system.

Carbon Dioxide Emissions

When geothermal power plants do emit gases, it's mostly carbon dioxide, which isn't a pollutant but a greenhouse gas. Still, geothermal power plants emit much less carbon dioxide than fossil fuel power plants.

Also, the common practice by geothermal power plants to inject geothermal fluids back into reservoirs to sustain resources has diminished their carbon dioxide emissions. Carbon dioxide emissions from the Dixie Valley geothermal "flash" power plant in Nevada decreased 39 percent when it started using this practice in 1992.

Hydrogen Sulfide Emissions

Gases released from geothermal fluids may also include hydrogen sulfide, which causes the characteristic sulfurous odor often evident near natural hot springs. But typical emissions of hydrogen sulfide from geothermal power plants are less than 1 part per billion—well below what people can smell. In fact, most geothermal power plants produce such low concentrations of hydrogen sulfide that they require no special controls to comply with most state and federal emission standards. However, at The Geysers in California, the steam contains up to 0.15 percent hydrogen sulfide by weight, but treatment processes remove more than 99.9 percent of emissions.

As a result of the hydrogen sulfide treatment processes at The Geysers, Lake County became the first and only county in compliance with California's stringent air quality regulations in 1990. The State of California has also honored Pacific Gas & Electric Company (initial owner) and Calpine Corporation (present owner) for air pollution prevention at The Geysers. Calpine also received the 2004 Clean Air Award for Technology Development from the American Lung Associations of the Bay Area. . . .

Pipes tap into underground thermal steam at a power plant near the Salton Sea in California's Imperial Valley.

Minimizing Solid Waste and Recovering Minerals

Although many geothermal power plants generate no appreciable solid waste, the unique characteristics of some geothermal fluids require special attention to handle entrained solid byproducts.

Interestingly, these solid byproducts often contain valuable minerals that can be recovered and recycled for other industrial uses.

At the Salton Sea geothermal power plants in southern California, the mineralized geothermal brine contains enough corrosive salts and heavy metals to require special disposal. To remove the heavy metals, the plants dewater the waste stream. The salts are crystallized and removed. The remaining solids contain mostly silica, which is removed for use as a valuable raw material in several industrial processes.

Valuable minerals and metals can even be recovered via the hydrogen sulfide treatment systems at The Geysers in northern California. One system converts the hydrogen sulfide into elemental sulfur, which is recycled for use as a feedstock for sulfuric acid production.

U.S. Department of Energy (DOE) laboratories continue to research and develop better ways to recover and recycle minerals. . . .

Meeting Water Quality Standards

U.S. geothermal power plants can easily meet federal, state, and local water quality and conservation standards.

U.S. geothermal power plants use cooling towers or air-cooled condensers to reject waste heat into the atmosphere.

Huge cooling towers spew steam at The Geysers geothermal power plant in northern California, an area rich in geothermal activity.

The Environmental Advantages of Geothermal Energy

Geothermal energy use has a net positive environmental impact. Geothermal power plants have fewer and more easily controlled atmospheric emissions than either fossil fuel or nuclear plants. Direct heat uses are even cleaner and are practically non-polluting when compared to conventional heating. Another advantage, which differentiates geothermal energy from other renewables, is its continuous availability, 24 hours a day all year round.

World Energy Council, "Survey of Energy Resources." www.worldenergy.org.

Therefore, unlike most fossil fuel and nuclear power plants, they dump no waste heat into rivers or surface water. Waste heat can disrupt biota, such as algae and fish, in local water bodies.

Technology for the safe, nonpolluting use of geothermal fluids has been carefully developed and rigorously tested. Geothermal production and injection wells are lined with steel or titanium casing and cement to isolate fluids from the environment, including groundwater. Repeated examination—using sonic logging instruments and videography—of the casing and cement ensures that no leakage occurs. Spent geothermal fluids are then injected back into the reservoirs from which they were drawn. This solves the fluid disposal problem. It also prolongs the use of the geothermal reservoirs because it replenishes the fluids. . . .

Minimizing Land Use and Impact

For energy production and development, geothermal power plants don't use much land compared to coal and nuclear power plants. And the environmental impact upon the land they use is minimal.

An entire geothermal field uses 1–8 acres per megawatt (MW) versus 5–10 acres per MW for nuclear operations and 19 acres per MW for coal power plants. Coal power plants also require huge acreages for mining their fuel. These mining operations can involve large-scale movement of earth for construction of underground mine shafts and tunnels, waste heaps, and/or open pits. Disturbed surfaces from open pit mining also can limit plant life participation in the carbon cycle and evapotranspiration [the loss of water by evaporation through soil and transpiration from plants], which replenishes water in the atmosphere. Adequate remediation of strip-mined areas can be expensive too.

A typical geothermal power plant requires wells, and drilling them impacts the land. However, advanced directional or slant drilling technology has evolved, which minimizes the impact. This drilling technology allows several wells to be drilled from one location. This reduces the amount of land needed for drilling pads, access roads, and geothermal fluid piping.

For geothermal exploration, slimhole drilling can be used to minimize environmental impact. Slimhole wells are only 4–6 inches in diameter, while traditional geothermal exploration wells have been 8–12 inches in diameter. Slimhole drilling also reduces the amount of land needed for site preparation and road construction.

Subsidence

Land subsidence can occur following the withdrawal of large amounts of fluid—water, oil, and even geothermal fluid—from beneath the earth's surface. The common practice by geothermal power plants to inject spent geothermal fluids back into reservoirs to sustain resources helps prevent subsidence from occurring.

Geothermal Energy Harms the Environment

Robert L. Bradley Jr.

Robert L. Bradley Jr. asserts in this selection that geothermal energy is not a renewable source as many claim. Although worldwide reserves are so vast they may seem unlimited and renewable, in fact, geothermal reservoirs can be depleted if more steam is extracted than is injected or naturally replenished. Other problems are associated with geothermal energy as well, argues Bradley. The most serious is geothermal energy plants' negative impact on the environment. These plants produce carbon dioxide and hydrogen sulfide emissions as well as toxic waste. Bradley is president of the Institute for Energy Research and the author of the two-volume Oil, Gas, and Government: The U.S. Experience. *He is also an adjunct scholar at the Cato Institute, a libertarian public policy research organization.*

A multi-billion-dollar government crusade to promote renewable energy for electricity generation, now in its third decade, has resulted in major economic costs and unintended environmental consequences. Even improved new generation renewable capacity is, on average, *twice* as expensive as new capacity from the most economical fossil-fuel alternative and *triple* the cost of surplus electricity. Solar power for bulk generation is substantially more uneconomic

Energy Sources Used in the United States

Renewable Sources		Percentage of Total Power Generated
Hydroelectric	Turbines in dams spin using water power.	**7%**
Biomass	Wood and wood waste are burned or turned into liquid fuel.	**.97%**
Landfill waste and gas	Trash and the methane gas it creates can be burned as fuel.	**.61%**
Geothermal	Hot water and steam provide power to turbine engines.	**.37%**
Solar	Panels collect energy from the sun.	**.01%**
Wind	Turbines in spinning windmills collect energy.	**.29%**

Compare to These Nonrenewable Energy Sources		
Fossil fuels	Oil, coal, and natural gas are finite fuel sources created millions of years ago.	**71%**
Nuclear	The type of uranium (metal) used as atom-splitting fuel is nonrenewable and somewhat rare.	**20%**

Source: Energy Information Administration, U.S. Department of Energy (www.eia.doe.gov), 2005.

than the average; biomass, hydroelectric power, and geothermal projects are less uneconomic. Wind power is the closest to the double-triple rule.

Renewables Harm the Environment

The uncompetitiveness of renewable generation explains the emphasis pro-renewable energy lobbyists on both the state and federal levels put on quota requirements, as well as continued or expanded subsidies. Yet every major renewable energy source has drawn criticism from leading environmental groups: hydro

Tim Eagan. © 2004 Tim Eagan. Reproduced by permission.

for river habitat destruction, wind for avian mortality, solar for desert overdevelopment, biomass for air emissions, and geothermal for depletion and toxic discharges.

Current state and federal efforts to restructure the electricity industry are being politicized to foist a new round of involuntary commitments on ratepayers and taxpayers for politically favored renewables, particularly wind and solar. Yet new government subsidies for favored renewable technologies are likely to create few environmental benefits; increase electricity-generation overcapacity in most regions of the United States; raise electricity rates; and create new "environmental pressures," given the extra land and materials (compared with those needed for traditional technologies) it would take to significantly increase the capacity of wind and solar generation.

One of the centerpieces of the environmentalist agenda has long been the regulation of fossil-fuel consumption. Although anti-pollution controls are the accepted short-term solution to many of the environmental problems posed by fossil fuels, many people believe that the long-term answer is the gradual replacement of fossil fuels with other, less environmentally threatening fuel sources. That philosophy can perhaps best be described as eco-energy planning, the belief that government intervention in the energy economy is necessary to maximize environmental protection and, in the end, the nation's economic vitality.

Not-So-Promising Alternatives

Renewable energy—power generated from the nearly infinite elements of nature such as sunshine, wind, the movement of water, the internal heat of the Earth, and the combustion of replenishable crops—is widely popular with the public and governmental officials because it is thought to be an inexhaustible and environmentally benign source of power, particularly compared with the supposedly finite and environmentally problematic alternative of reliance on fossil fuels and nuclear power. Renewable energy is the centerpiece of eco-energy planning. Yet all renewable energy sources are not created equal. Some are more economically and environmentally viable than others. The list of renewable fuels that were once promising but are now being questioned on economic or environmental grounds, or both, is growing.

Wind power is currently the environmentalists' favorite source of renewable energy and is thought be the most likely renewable energy source to replace fossil fuel in the generation of electricity in the 21st century. Hydropower has lost favor with environmentalists because of the damage it has done to river habitats and freshwater fish populations. Solar power, at least when relied on for central-station or grid electricity generation, is not environmentally benign on a total fuel cycle basis and is highly uneconomic, land intensive, and thus a fringe electric power source for the foreseeable future. Geothermal has turned out to be "depletable," with limited capacity, falling output, and modest new investment. Biomass is also uneconomic and an air-pollution-intensive renewable. . . .

Geothermal: The Nonrenewable Renewable

Geothermal—steam energy that is generated by the Earth's heated core—is currently produced at 19 sites in four western states (California, Hawaii, Nevada, and Oregon) and accounts for just under 1/2 of 1 percent of national power production and national generation capacity. Production has fallen far short of projections made in the 1980s and is currently in decline because of erratic output from a number of California properties. Nationally, geothermal output in 1995 was 14 percent below 1994, a drop of 2.4 million kWh [kilowatt-hours].

The experience of the world's largest geothermal facility— the 1,672 MW [megawatt] facility known as the Geysers—is emblematic. As Pacific Gas and Electric reported,

> Because of declining geothermal steam supplies, the Company's geothermal units at The Geysers Power Plant are forecast to operate at reduced capacities. The consolidated Geysers capacity factor is forecast to be approximately 33 percent in 1995, which includes forced outages, scheduled overhaul and projected steam shortage curtailments, as compared to the actual Geysers capacity factor of

The Morning Glory thermal pool at Yellowstone National Park is an environmentally protected site. Its reservoirs cannot be tapped for commercial purposes.

56 percent in 1994. The Company expects steam supplies at the Geysers to continue to decline.

After reporting a 37 percent performance for 1995 (versus the 33 percent forecast), Pacific Gas and Electric predicted a lower percentage for 1996 due to "economic curtailments, forced outages, scheduled overhauls, and projected steam shortage curtailments."

Undesirable Sites for Geothermal Development

A number of drawbacks are inhibiting geothermal growth. Geothermal is site specific and may not match customer demand centers. Geothermal sites often are located in protected wilderness areas that environmentalists do not want disturbed. Unique reservoir characteristics and limited historical experience increase investor risk. Depletion occurs where more steam is withdrawn than is naturally recharged or injected, and "inexhaustible" reservoirs can become noncommercial. Alternative water uses or low availability have reduced recharging capacity at the Geysers, for example. Corrosive acids have also destroyed equipment at the facility, and toxic emissions can occur. Promising sites can turn into dry holes upon completion of drilling. Surplus gas-fired generation in California, New Mexico, and Utah also has removed the need for new geothermal capacity. Concluded one journalist [Arthur O'Donnell] conversant with the western U.S. renewable industry,

> By all accounts, the utility-grade geothermal power development business has reached a plateau within the United States. The few dozen viable sites identified and developed in California and Nevada during the 1980s are now entering a mature operational phase. New exploration opportunities—mainly in Oregon and northern California—are sparse due to high cost and perceived "overcapacity" of resources held by utilities. Even expansion of existing plants is limited because of the low avoided-cost energy prices currently available from utilities and the current restrictions on nonutility purchasers.

Depleting Source of Energy

Is geothermal a renewable resource? [A study by Christopher Flavin and Rick Piltz, "Sustainable Energy," 1989] included the statement that "geothermal is one of the few renewable energy sources that can be a reliable supplier of baseload electricity," yet the same study also noted that "geothermal resources are not strictly *renewable* on a human time scale, but the source is so vast it seems limitless." Flavin and Lenssen [said in their report, "Power Surge,"] . . . five years later, "Although geothermal reserves can be depleted if managed incorrectly (and in some cases have been), worldwide resources are sufficiently large for this energy resource to be treated as renewable." Yet the coal supply of the United States combined with the natural gas supply in North America is arguably "so vast it seems limitless" as well. Geothermal cannot be considered a renewable resource, at least in the United States.

Geothermal is not only a scarce, depleting resource, it has negative environmental consequences despite the absence of combustion. In some applications, there can be CO_2 [carbon dioxide] emissions, heavy requirements for cooling water (as much as 100,000 gal. per MW per day), hydrogen sulfide emissions, and waste disposal issues with dissolved solids, and even toxic waste. Those problems and the location problem have caused some environmental groups to withhold support for geothermal since the late 1980s.

CHAPTER 2

The Future of Geothermal Energy

Clouds of steam emerging from the Salton Sea geothermal power plant take on an eerie glow at dusk.

Geothermal Can Become an Important Energy Contributor

Charles F. Kutscher

Electric power generation from geothermal resources began in the United States in 1960, and today, more than twenty plants provide a total of twenty-two hundred megawatts of electricity, according to Charles F. Kutscher in this selection. Nevertheless, growth in the industry has been declining since the 1990s, due to depleted supplies, competition from relatively inexpensive natural gas, and lack of government incentives. To reduce the cost of geothermal electricity, the U.S. Department of Energy is researching more effective and less expensive ways to find and develop geothermal resources. With this renewed investment and increasing support for clean, renewable energy, geothermal energy will become an important power source in the future. Kutscher is a principal engineer at the National Renewable Energy Laboratory in Golden, Colorado.

Geothermal electricity production in the United States began in 1960. Today there are over 20 plants in the western United States providing a total of about 2,200 MW [megawatts] of clean and reliable electricity. Currently identified resources could provide over 20,000 MW of power in the U.S., and undiscovered resources might provide 5 times that amount.

In the 1990s industry growth slowed due to the loss of market incentives and competition from natural gas. However, increased interest in clean energy sources, ongoing technological

Charles F. Kutscher, "The Status and Future of Geothermal Electric Power," August 2000. National Renewable Energy Laboratory. Reproduced by permission.

improvements, and renewed opportunities abroad hold promise for a resurgence in the industry. . . .

Geothermal Use in the United States

Geothermal resources can be divided into four types: hydrothermal, geopressured, hot dry rock, and magma. Except for geothermal (or ground-source) heat pumps, which utilize the heat contained in shallow soil, all existing uses of geothermal energy make use of hydrothermal resources, which consist of some combination of hot water and steam located in permeable rock. The hot geothermal fluid is used for direct heating applications such as spas, greenhouses, district heating and the like. If the resource temperature is greater than about 90°C, it can be utilized to generate electricity. . . .

Currently, geothermal energy is used to generate a total of about 8,000 MW of electricity in 21 countries. The United States is the largest user with about 2,200 MW of current capacity. Most of the geothermal power in the United States is generated in California and Nevada with California accounting for over 90% of installed capacity. A considerable amount of this power (1,137 MW) is generated at The Geysers in Northern California, which has hosted a number of commercial geothermal power plants since the first one was built there in 1960. The Geysers . . . is a fairly unusual (and ideal) resource because its wells produce virtually pure steam with no water.

It has been estimated that identified hydrothermal resources in the United States could provide 23,000 MWe [megawatts of electricity] for 30 years, and undiscovered resources might provide 5 times that amount. If it were to become economic to tap into more widespread "hot dry rock" resources (which involves deeper drilling and injection of water to recover the heat), the U.S. geothermal energy resource would be sufficient to provide our current electric demand for tens of thousands of years.

Although steam plants tend to release some gases from the geothermal fluid, amounts are usually small, and there are suitable means for mitigating most of these releases. Thus, geothermal energy tends to be quite clean. In fact, Lake County, which is the location of The Geysers geothermal power plants, is

Geothermal Resources in the United States

Geothermal energy is tapped from heat below the earth's surface. This heat is everywhere, but the most desirable energy resources exist where the highest underground temperatures occur.

Most of the hottest regions are located in the same spots as active volcanoes. Many promising geothermal resources are in protected regions such as national parks and scenic or wilderness areas.

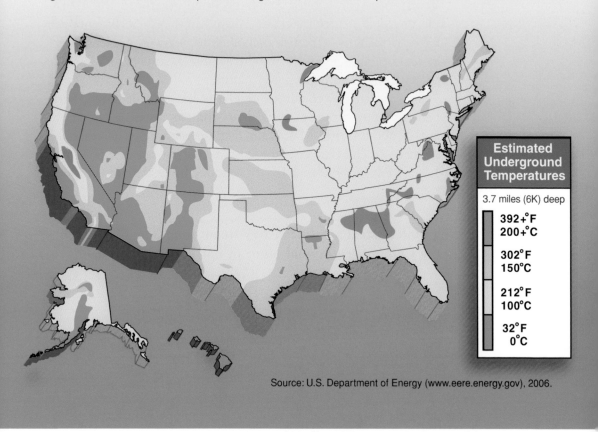

Estimated Underground Temperatures

3.7 miles (6K) deep

392+°F
200+°C

302°F
150°C

212°F
100°C

32°F
0°C

Source: U.S. Department of Energy (www.eere.energy.gov), 2006.

reported to be the only county in California that is in compliance with all of California's air quality regulations. . . .

Plans to Increase Output

Between 1980 and 1990, about 900 MWe of geothermal electric capacity were installed in the United States. Most of these plants were built in California and Nevada under power purchase agreements that guaranteed prices of more than 10 cents per kWh [kilowatt-hour]. Today, most of these price guarantees have expired, and plants must sell their power at competitive rates. With the loss of government market incentives, the advent of low-cost electricity from natural gas turbines, and the decline in electricity load growth, geothermal power plant construction in the United States declined greatly in the 1990s. Geothermal electricity costs, in the range of 5 to 8 cents per kWh, while very attractive compared to many other clean energy technologies, cannot compete against 3 cents per kWh electricity from natural gas power plants.

The actual power output of plants has also declined, with U.S. generation now at 2,200 MW compared with a rated output of about 2,800 MW. This decline is mostly the result of changes at The Geysers, where power output has dropped from 1,875 MW in 1990 to 1,137 MW today [in 2002]. This drop is

Stainless steel pipelines carry steam from The Geysers to the Calpine geothermal plant in northern California.

due both to the retirement of older plants and a loss in reservoir volume over the years.

To address the reservoir depletion problem, two projects have been initiated to inject reclaimed wastewater into the reservoir. The first phase of the Southeast Geysers Effluent System has recently been completed. This transports 20,500 L/min [liters/minute] (5,400 gallons per minute) of wastewater from several Lake County communities to The Geysers via a 30 mile pipeline. This has enhanced steam production and increased power output by 39 MW between January 1998 and January 1999. A second phase of that project is planned, and there is a plan to transport wastewater from the City of Santa Rosa a distance of 41 miles to The Geysers. These projects not only prolong the lifetime of the geothermal resource but also provide a solution to wastewater disposal problems.

As a result of the unfavorable economic conditions for geothermal energy in the United States, the industry has looked for opportunities abroad. Good opportunities for geothermal power plants exist in many developing countries, where the Geothermal Energy Association has estimated there is the potential for approximately 75,000 MW of capacity for 30 years. Especially attractive are Central America (22,000 MW), Indonesia (16,000 MW), East Africa (10,000 MW), and the Philippines (8,000 MW). Considerable new activity was underway in the Philippines and Indonesia until the Asian economic crisis put many planned geothermal power plant construction projects on hold.

Current Research Activities

The Department of Energy research program is aimed at reducing the cost of geothermal electricity. This involves research in the following areas:

Exploration research focuses on developing more accurate and lower cost means for finding and mapping geothermal resources. In this way the financial risk of developing a project can be minimized. Reservoir research is aimed at maximizing the production rate and lifetime of the geothermal resource. Both areas involve the development of improved computer models and better instrumentation. Recent accomplishments include development of instrumentation that can work in higher-temperature environments and more accurate field survey procedures.

The *cost of drilling* a well can be a significant portion of the overall plant cost. Drilling research has focused on means to reduce the costs of drilling through hard rock in high-temperature, corrosive environments. Recent accomplishments include the development of slimhole drilling that reduces costs by up to 50% and improved drilling control and tools.

Energy conversion research is aimed at reducing the delivered electricity cost by improving performance, lowering equipment cost, and reducing O&M [operation and maintenance] costs of geothermal power plants. Because geothermal power plants operate at relatively low temperatures compared to other power plants, thermodynamics dictates that they reject to the environment as much as 90% of the heat extracted out of the ground. Research has thus focused on improving the heat rejection equipment, and new designs of both water-cooled and air-cooled condensers have been developed. Other research accomplishments include improved thermodynamic cycles that extract more energy out of each kilogram of brine, better maintenance techniques, and the development of heat exchanger linings that protect low-cost heat exchanger materials from corrosion and scaling when subjected to geothermal fluids.

The Future of the Geothermal Industry

Operators of existing plants are working hard to lower O&M costs in order to improve their profit margins now that price guarantees for many plants have expired. The need to reduce labor costs has produced a trend toward more automation. Plant owners are also actively looking at ways to improve plant efficiency and, in some cases, are adjusting plant operation to accommodate a resource that is declining with time.

In some cases, totally new power plant concepts are being considered. For example, one company is exploring use of the Kalina cycle, a binary cycle that utilizes a mixture of ammonia and water as the working fluid. This cycle has the potential to

Using diamond-studded drill bits (inset), a rig searches for new steam wells near The Geysers facility. Exploratory drilling is costly and problematic.

extract a third more energy from the geothermal fluid than a conventional cycle.

There are a number of reasons to believe that the economic climate may improve. The movement toward consumer disclosure, associated with utility restructuring, will likely favor all clean energy sources, including geothermal. Portfolio standards aimed at requiring that a certain percentage of electric power generation must come from clean sources, and "green marketing" will also help make geothermal more attractive.

New Power Plant Development

Combining geothermal power production with other processes may provide sufficient financial incentives to make plants

Geothermal Power Plants in the United States

Geothermal power plants are located in the western part of the country, where the highest underground temperatures are found. In addition to the plant locations below, 45 new geothermal power plants are under development in the United States. The new plants will nearly double U.S. geothermal power output.

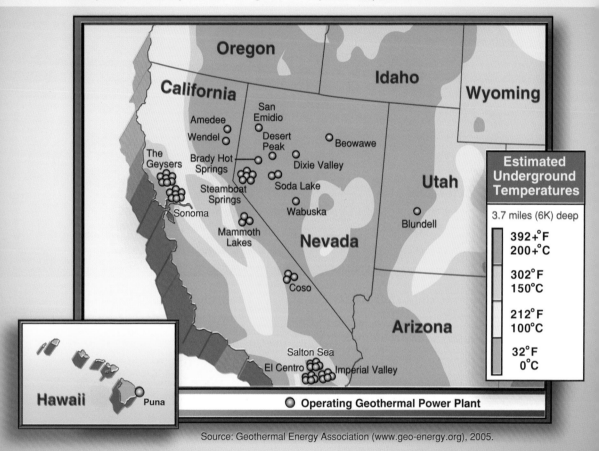

Source: Geothermal Energy Association (www.geo-energy.org), 2005.

economic. For example, a new plant at the Salton Sea in California extracts zinc from highly saline brine that is also used to generate electric power.

In addition to new plant development at the Salton Sea, there are two new proposed 50-MW plants at Glass Mountain, California, being done under a California Energy Commission program. According to [the report "Geothermal Electric Power Production in the United States: A Survey and Update for

1995–1999"], there are plans for a total additional U.S. geothermal electric capacity of 578 MW over the next five years, although it is not clear how much of this will actually be built. As Asia emerges from its economic crisis, the geothermal industry there is expected to pick up again. A number of opportunities in Latin America and Africa are also being pursued.

In order to improve the cost-effectiveness of small geothermal power plants, the U.S. Department of Energy, as part of a new Geopowering the West initiative, has released a Request for Proposals entitled "Field Verification of Small-Scale Geothermal Power Plants." Through this solicitation, DOE hopes to build several power plants in the size range of 300 kW to 1 MW. Data on performance and O&M costs will be collected for a three-year period, after which it is intended that the plants will continue to generate electricity for sale to the grid or to provide power for a local process. Additional solicitations will be aimed at improved drilling and enhancing the recovery of energy from existing geothermal reservoirs.

Geothermal electricity has already proven itself to be a clean, reliable, and comparatively inexpensive alternative to fossil fuels. Continued government-funded research in exploration and reservoirs, drilling, and energy conversion, performed in close collaboration with industry, offers considerable promise for significantly lowering the cost of geothermal power production. Combined with deployment programs and environmentally sensitive energy policies, geothermal can become a major energy contributor throughout the western United States and in many countries around the world.

Government Incentives Will Spur Geothermal Energy Use

National Renewable Energy Laboratory

The National Renewable Energy Laboratory reports in this selection that new federal and state policies will promote geothermal energy use and development. For example, many western states such as California and Nevada are mandating that utilities generate a certain percent of electricity from geothermal energy by the mid-2000s. The federal government offers incentives such as tax credits, clean renewable energy bonds, and loan programs to businesses in order to spur investment in geothermal energy. Homeowners benefit as well, as they are now eligible for a three-hundred-dollar tax credit for installing a geothermal heat pump. The National Renewable Energy Laboratory, part of the U.S. Department of Energy, aims to secure an energy future that is environmentally and economically sustainable.

National, state, and local energy policy has been a rapidly evolving area recently. Within the last few years, numerous policies and regulatory actions have had a profoundly positive impact on the development and market acceptance of renewable energy technologies, including geothermal.

There are many policy options for geothermal energy development, such as grant and loan programs; corporate, sales, and

National Renewable Energy Laboratory, "New Policies Have Favorable Impact on Geothermal Development," *Geothermal Today*, September 2005, pp. 32–36. Reproduced by permission.

property tax incentives; and 'green power' purchasing and mandatory utility requirements. Two policy concepts being implemented at the state level are renewable portfolio standards (RPS) and public benefit funds (PBF).

Renewable Energy Requirements

Twenty-two states and the District of Columbia have set legal deadlines for utility companies to generate a certain portion of the state's electricity from renewable sources.

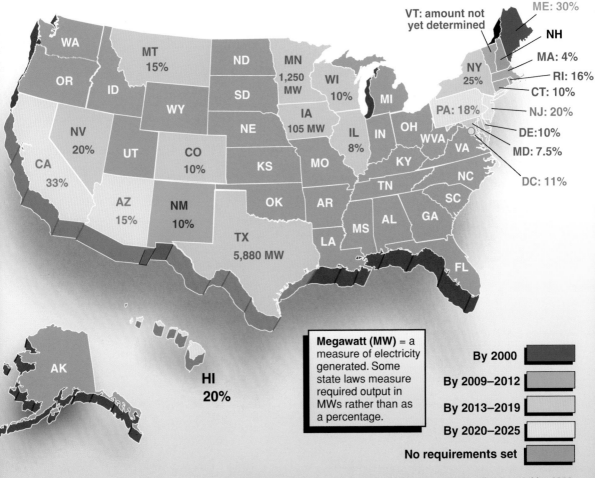

VT: amount not yet determined

ME: 30%

NH

MA: 4%

RI: 16%

CT: 10%

NJ: 20%

DE:10%

MD: 7.5%

DC: 11%

NY 25%

PA: 18%

WA

MT 15%

ND

MN 1,250 MW

WI 10%

MI

OR

ID

SD

IA 105 MW

IL 8%

IN

OH

WVA

VA

NV 20%

UT

WY

NE

CA 33%

CO 10%

KS

MO

KY

TN

NC

AZ 15%

NM 10%

OK

AR

SC

MS

AL

GA

TX 5,880 MW

LA

FL

AK

HI 20%

Megawatt (MW) = a measure of electricity generated. Some state laws measure required output in MWs rather than as a percentage.

By 2000

By 2009–2012

By 2013–2019

By 2020–2025

No requirements set

Source: The Pew Center on Global Climate Change (www.pewclimate.org), May 2006.

State Activity and Interest

RPS policies create mandates for states or specific utilities to generate a percent of electricity from renewable sources. Typically, a state decides how to fulfill this mandate using a combination of renewable energy sources, including wind, solar, biomass, and geothermal, or other renewable sources. Some RPS policies specify the technology mix, while others leave it up to the market. States may even include energy efficiency improvements as part of their 'clean power' require-

President George W. Bush signs the Energy Policy Act of 2005. The bill aims to lessen American dependency on foreign oil sources.

ments. Hawaii, Illinois, and Minnesota apply voluntary RPS policies, as another option.

To date, 21 states and Washington, D.C., have implemented minimum RPS or generation targets, including several in western states with known geothermal potential. For example, California, with the fifth largest economy in the world, has enacted a requirement of 20 percent by 2017. In fact, a recent RPS integration study done for the California Energy Commission indicated that geothermal resources would contribute the most toward reaching this goal. Nevada, called the Saudi Arabia of geothermal resources by U.S. Senator Harry Reid, has a 20 percent requirement (which includes energy efficiency) by 2013. Some of the other western states with RPS policies are Montana with a 15 percent requirement by 2015 and New Mexico with a 10 percent requirement by 2010.

PBF policies are typically state-level programs developed through the electric utility restructuring process to assure continued support for renewable energy resources, energy efficiency initiatives, and low-income support programs. These funds are also frequently referred to as a system benefits charge. Such a fund is commonly supported through a charge to all customers on electricity consumption. . . . Examples of how the funds are used include: rebates on renewable energy systems, funding for renewable energy R&D [research and development], and development of renewable energy education programs. To date, 15 states and Washington, D.C., have PBF policies, including several western states with known geothermal potential, such as Arizona, California, Oregon, and Montana.

National Activity and Interest

The new 2005 Energy Bill recently passed by Congress and signed by President Bush on August 8, 2005, previously included a 10 percent national RPS, however, it was removed in a joint conference committee vote. Measure sponsors will reintroduce RPS legislation, and we may yet see a national RPS.

This new legislation contains some noteworthy and substantial incentives for geothermal development. These will be briefly described below.

Production Tax Credit—A 1.9 cents/kWh [kilowatt-hour] credit is in place, and developers may claim this credit for ten years instead of only five years, as was the case until the new energy legislation went into effect. The generation facility must be "placed in service" by December 31, 2007.

Utility Cooperatives—This provision allows cooperatives to pass any portion of the renewable electricity production credit to their members, thus sharing financial incentives with investors. An eligible cooperative is defined as a cooperative organization that is owned more than 50 percent by agricultural producers or entities owned by agricultural producers.

Bonds, Royalties, and Leases

Clean Renewable Energy Bonds—This provision creates a new Clean Renewable Energy Bond (CREB) to provide cooperatives, other not-for-profit electric companies, and Indian Tribal governments incentives for building new geothermal and other qualified energy projects. Provision is effective for bonds issued after December 31, 2005.

Simplifying the Law

The bill streamlines some of the most bureaucratic aspects of the law. It simplifies the royalty payment requirements, provides clear direction for the agencies to make geothermal use a priority, gives local governments more funding to mitigate impacts, and ensures that the federal agencies will have the resources needed to implement the new law and quickly work-off a backlog of unfinished studies and lease applications.

In regards to royalties, before this new law, the federal and state governments equally split royalty payments that companies pay when they lease public lands for geothermal power. Now, the states will receive half the royalty income, with the federal and county governments each receiving 25 percent. And as Churchill County (Nevada) Commissioner Norman Frey says, "For a small county like Churchill, it's a big deal." The new 25 percent split could mean about $1.5 million for

Churchill County, which could go toward the library or senior center, according to Commissioner Frey.

Direct users of geothermal energy (non-electric uses) may also use a simpler procedure for leasing on federal lands and establishing a fee schedule instead of royalty payments. State and local governments are now allowed to use geothermal resources for public purposes at a nominal charge. This could lead to substantial geothermal direct uses, such as district heating, while achieving significant financial savings on supplanted conventional energy costs.

Tax Credits and Rebates

Geothermal Heat Pumps—One of the highlights of the new bill addresses homeowners, who are granted up to $300 in tax credits (Sec. 1333) for the cost of new geothermal heat pumps

A geothermal heat pump (left) is used at a commercial facility in 1996. At right, in 2001, a geothermal heat pump and water heater are used in a Virginia residence.

Tax Incentives Make Geothermal Energy More Competitive

Now, geothermal power plants qualify for the same tax incentives as wind facilities—a 1.9 cent [per kilowatt-hour] credit for the first ten years of production—making geothermal power costs more competitive.

Alyssa Kagel and Karl Gawell, *Institutional Investor*, December 2005.

(GHP—sometimes called ground-source heat pumps) systems. To be eligible, certain performance and energy efficiency standards must be met. However, the system must include a 'desuperheater' or integrated water heating to meet the credit's criteria. There are also provisions for residential tax credits and commercial tax deductions for energy efficient building, and this could include the use of GHPs. According to the Geothermal Heat Pump Consortium, an industry group, there are 22 states that offer tax incentives for GHPs. You can check to see if your state offers incentives at: *www.geoexchange.org/incentives/incentives.htm*.

The section covering renewable energy security offers a 25 percent rebate, up to $3,000, for renewable energy systems that "(i) when installed in connection with a dwelling, transmits or uses— (I) solar energy, energy derived from the geothermal deposits, energy derived from biomass, or any other form of renewable energy which the Secretary specifies by regulations, for the purpose of heating or cooling such dwelling or providing hot water or electricity for use within such dwelling. . ." The GHP industry is now working to ensure GHP technology is not excluded from this definition, which could bring an even greater interest to geothermal technology.

Research and Development Initiative

R&D Direction—The 2005 Energy Bill's Title IX, *Research and Development*, includes provisions directing DOE to continue a geothermal research program, providing specific goals for that effort. The bill language stipulates:

GEOTHERMAL. The Secretary shall conduct a program of research, development, demonstration, and commercial application for geothermal energy. The program shall focus on developing improved technologies for reducing the costs of geothermal energy installations, including technologies for:

- Improving detection of geothermal resources
- Decreasing drilling costs
- Decreasing maintenance costs through improved materials
- Increasing the potential for other revenue sources, such as mineral production, and
- Increasing the understanding of reservoir life cycle and management."

Further, the 2005 Energy Bill revised the Geothermal Steam Act and directs the U.S. Geological Survey to submit an updated nationwide geothermal resource assessment to Congress within three years. There hasn't been a nationwide geothermal resource assessment in nearly 30 years.

New Technology May Allow Geothermal Energy Development Anywhere on Earth

Nolan Fell

This selection by science journalist Nolan Fell describes new geothermal heat extraction technology. Traditionally, a dual-well system is used, which can only tap geothermal resources near those geological features that are close to Earth's surface. In this system, two pipes are necessary—one to extract hot water from the geothermal fissure and one to return cold water back into the ground. Today, scientists in Aachen, Germany, are developing a new system that some experts think will allow for drilling anywhere on Earth. This approach uses a single pipe that can bore down 2.5 kilometers into the ground. Hot water is extracted and cold water injected through this single pipe. Fell is a science and technology journalist from London.

The people of Aachen in western Germany are no strangers to hot water bubbling up from deep inside the Earth. The city was built on a hot spring and is still renowned for its spa. But Aachen may soon have another source of hot water to be proud of. A team of geologists and engineers hopes to sink a huge borehole in the city centre and show the world that geothermal heating is there for the taking, anywhere on the planet.

Nolan Fell, "Deep Heat," *New Scientist*, Vol. 177, February 22, 2003, p. 40.

The idea of using the Earth's natural warmth to heat homes and businesses is an old one. As early as 1910, steam from hot aquifers in and around Larderello in Tuscany was used to heat buildings and greenhouses. And in 1928 Iceland began using its geothermal hot water for central heating. Today, geothermal heating is used in 58 countries worldwide, according to the International Geothermal Association.

Old Technology Had Limited Benefits

Heat from the Earth has obvious attractions. It is free, clean, and abundant. Yet despite a century of development, its contribution to the world's heating bill remains negligible. The problem is that extracting heat has only been possible where unusual geological features push hot water or steam close to the Earth's surface.

Hot aquifers, for example, can be tapped using something called dual-well technology: you drill two boreholes, one to extract the hot water and the other to return it once it has cooled down. But such geological features are few and far between, and it is very rare for large populations to live on top of one—an absolute must for geothermal heating because you cannot transport heat long distances.

Problems with Geothermal Energy

Engineers have attempted to overcome this limitation using the "hot dry rock" method. The idea is to make an artificial hot aquifer by drilling two boreholes into deep rocks then fracturing the rock between them so water can percolate from one to the other. Then you can pump cold water down one borehole and extract it hot from the other.

Hot dry rock can work, but it is expensive and failure is common. Most countries are abandoning it, or looking to use unusual geological features, which rather defeats the object. In Sweden, for example, geologists are investigating the possibility of extracting heat from pre-fissured rock under the Björkö impact crater close to Stockholm.

Shallow geothermal systems have also been developed to extract heat from around 100 metres down. They are more common under new houses, but the heat they produce is low grade and requires an electric heat pump to concentrate it. Although they do cut heating bills, their environmental impact is minimal.

Economics has also played a part in holding back geothermal heat. Following the oil shocks of 1973 there was a surge of interest and the European Union backed a series of projects but support fizzled out in the 1980s as oil became cheap again.

New Deep Geothermal Heat-Exchanger Technology

Still the idea of tapping the ground for its abundant heat hasn't gone away. All over the globe, the temperature of the crust increases the deeper you go, typically by 30 to 33°C per kilometre. Surely there must be a reliable and economical way of extracting this heat wherever it is needed? That's what the Aachen project hopes to prove.

The technology at its heart is called a deep geothermal heat-exchanger, which consists of a single borehole sunk 2.5 kilometres into the Earth's crust. The hole will act as both source and sink—cold water in, hot water out. That makes it simpler and more reliable than a hot dry rock system. And according to the consortium of architects and engineering firms behind the project, you could install one under any building anywhere in the world.

Deep geothermal heat-exchangers already exist, but haven't quite taken the world by storm. The first was built—somewhat by accident—in Prenzlau in northeastern Germany several years ago. It was intended to be a hot dry rock system but the second borehole failed, and the designers had to dream up a way of exploiting a single borehole. The exchanger they put in produces heat, although nowhere near as much as intended. Since then three more deep geothermal heat-exchangers have been built, all in Switzerland. All three appear to be a success but none has released any public information so they have yet to inspire copycats.

Aachen Will Be Different

Aachen will be different. It is intended to demonstrate the value of the technology to a sceptical world. "We want to show

Hot Dry Rock (HDR) Technology

Where hot-water reservoirs do not occur naturally, hot rock can still be used to generate power.

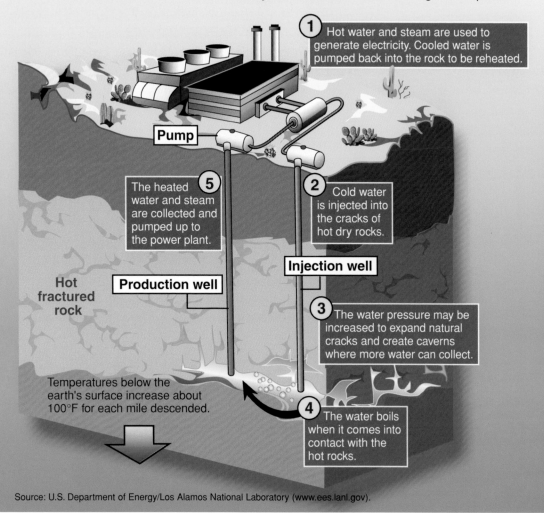

1 Hot water and steam are used to generate electricity. Cooled water is pumped back into the rock to be reheated.

Pump

5 The heated water and steam are collected and pumped up to the power plant.

2 Cold water is injected into the cracks of hot dry rocks.

Injection well

Production well

Hot fractured rock

3 The water pressure may be increased to expand natural cracks and create caverns where more water can collect.

Temperatures below the earth's surface increase about 100°F for each mile descended.

4 The water boils when it comes into contact with the hot rocks.

Source: U.S. Department of Energy/Los Alamos National Laboratory (www.ees.lanl.gov).

that the project is applicable anywhere," says Roland Gaschnitz of the Institute of Mine Surveying at the Technical University of Aachen, who is overseeing the technical issues surrounding the drilling and heat-extraction.

But surely Aachen's hot spring is exactly the kind of geological oddity the proponents of geothermal heating need to get away from? Not so, according to Gaschnitz. "The hot springs are 500 metres away, but there is a big geological fault between us and the spring," he says. As a result, the ground they will drill into probably has a normal thermal gradient, give or take a few degrees.

"There are two possibilities," Gaschnitz explains. "The water may help us by heating up the rocks a bit, and we might get more heat than we expect. But the crust is also thickened here. It is part of the Rheinisch Massif, a hilly region where two continents collided 200 million years ago. This might mean that the thermal gradient is slightly lower than normal. We will see."

Drilling is scheduled to begin in July [2003]. Within three months the hole should be 2.5 kilometres deep, reaching rock where the temperature is at least 80°C. Once the borehole is finished, a large building called SuperC will be erected on top of it. This will be the university's central hub with offices, conference rooms, and a cafe. The borehole will provide all the

Seen under construction in 2000, this office building in Maryland will incorporate energy-efficient systems such as solar panels and geothermal energy for heating and cooling.

heat the building needs in winter, as well as enough energy to cool it in summer. By replacing fossil-fuel energy, the Aachen team reckon the borehole can reduce the University's CO_2 emissions by 380 tonnes a year. . . .

In the winter, hot water from the heat-exchanger will be piped through the building's walls, floors, and ceilings to keep it at a toasty 22°C. The spent water will then flow back into the heat-exchanger. During the summer, the hot water will be fed into an air-conditioning system called an adsorption cooler. This works by evaporating water under a near-vacuum, cooling the air just as an alcohol swab cools the skin. And when the weather is mild the building can be kept comfortable by reducing the volume of water flowing through the heat-exchanger.

Iceland Shows How Geothermal Energy Can Help Nations Reduce Dependence on Oil

Barbara Eaglesham

In the following selection Barbara Eaglesham explains that the volcanic island of Iceland uniquely benefits from geothermal activity. Geothermal energy provides Iceland with heated water that can be tapped for numerous public works projects that increase the quality of life on the frigid island. Iceland began exploiting its geothermal resources during the 1920s, when it used geothermal heat to warm greenhouses to grow a variety of food crops, thus ending its dependence on imported fruits and vegetables. Since then, projects using geothermal energy have included the heating of homes, businesses, schools, and hospitals, Eaglesham reports. Today, geothermal energy heats 85 percent of homes in Iceland and saves the country $100 million in imported oil each year. Eaglesham is a science writer for *Odyssey* magazine.

Y ou might not consider living astride a string of volcanoes to be cause for celebration. Icelanders do, though, and they are sharing their secret with the world: geothermal energy, also known as heat from the Earth. Hot underground natural reservoirs supply water to heat their homes, fill their swimming pools, let them grow much of their own food, and help them create products for export. The result of all this is a standard of living among the highest in the world, and clean air, too!

Not a New Idea

The geothermal energy idea isn't exactly new. For centuries, "hot springs" . . . were used on a small scale throughout the world as places to bathe and "take the cure" for aches and pains. The thermae in Herculaneum and Pompeii are examples. In 13th-century Iceland, poet and saga writer Snorri Sturluson built a wooden conduit to transport water from a thermal spring (*hver* in Icelandic) to a circular pool at his farm, Reykholt (reyk equals steam plume and holt means hill). Hot springs are still used in the same manner today.

The idea of actively harnessing the Earth's heat and putting it to work with modern methods didn't take hold until 1913, however. The world's first geothermal electric power station, driven by energy from natural steam, was constructed in Tuscany in northern Italy at that time. Less than 10 years later, in the 1920s, Iceland ended its great dependence on imported food (and provided islanders with something more exciting to eat than locally grown potatoes and fish) with the pioneering development of geothermally heated greenhouses. Suddenly, lettuce, tomatoes, and eggplant were available at reasonable prices.

Finally, in 1930, Iceland broadened the concept to include the large-scale heating of homes and businesses, known as district heating. A pilot program in the capital city, Reykjavik (pronounced RAY-kjah-veek), brought hot water from springs and shallow wells on the outskirts of town to a school, hospital, two public swimming pools, and about 70 homes. The program was so successful that it was soon expanded. By the time the oil crisis arrived in the 1970s, half the population of Iceland was already being served with low-cost heating. Rising oil prices created the incentive to expand the program further, and now 85 percent of all homes in Iceland are heated by this method. Where does all this heat come from? . . .

The capital city of Iceland, Reykjavik is entirely powered by geothermal energy, thanks to its abundant underground steam wells.

Extracting Heat from the Earth

Iceland is a volcanic island . . . born of magma rising from the splitting crusts of the Mid-Atlantic Ridge. (Think of the ridge that rises in the middle of a pound cake after the heat of baking causes the cake to expand and split down the middle—this process is ongoing in a volcanic ridge.) This assures Iceland all of the four necessary geological ingredients for the production and retention of a hot underground reservoir, known as a field. The ingredients form a kind of sandwich, with the bottom layer being a source of heat (in this case, hot volcanic rock). Lying over that is a layer of bedrock. Over the bedrock is an aquifer, a large volume of water within permeable rock that acts as a reservoir. Lastly, there is a lid to hold in the heat and vapor, a near-solid rock cap.

The process works like this: Heat flows from the source by conduction through the bedrock. In addition, intensely hot gases and vapor shoot through faults and fissures in the bedrock, and help to heat the aquifer water. The temperature in the aquifer rises by convection as the water circulates. With the rise in temperature comes expansion of the water, and the increase in volume forces some water to the surface through openings in the rock cap above the aquifer. . . .

Water can emerge from the ground in a gentle manner, in the case of lower temperature, lower pressure, semithermal fields (with water temperatures under 100 degrees C.). Or, it can gush forth as geysers, as is the case with hyperthermal fields (with water temperatures over 100 degrees C.) . . . For such a system to sustain itself, there must be an influx of water to replace that which is lost. Precipitation trickling into the ground accomplishes this.

In Iceland, low-temperature water (80 degrees C.) is pumped from deep wells (5,002,000 meters) to the surface by pumps located at depths of 100 to 250 meters. The water is stored in insulated tanks, which help to accommodate periods of high demand. . . .

A 1,179-km-long network of pipes carries water from 60 wells in Reykjavik to 99.9 percent of the city's population—around 160,000 people. Low-temperature water is also used as a drying agent in industrial processes such as the purification of salt, in fish farming, and in heating greenhouses.

Benefits Include Year-Round Swimming and Therapeutic Waters

You might not guess that an island with more than its fair share of glaciers would also have more than its fair share of open-air swimming pools. But there are 120 public pools in Iceland, and swimming instruction is mandatory in grade school. If it weren't for geothermally heated waters, swimming

FACTS TO CONSIDER

The Iceland Deep Drilling Project Could Produce Groundbreaking Amounts of Energy

This winter [2005], a group of scientists who work for several Icelandic energy companies are launching the Iceland Deep Drilling Project. The project aims to drill to a depth of 5 kilometers (3 miles) and extract water that has become a supercritical fluid. A supercritical fluid is a substance under high temperature and pressure that is neither a liquid nor a gas but something in between. A supercritical fluid holds much more heat than steam does, so a supercritical well could yield far more geothermal energy than any of Iceland's current wells.

Emma Davy, *Current Science*, February 11, 2005.

How Geysers Work

Geyers are hot springs that repeatedly burst into fountains of boiling water and steam. Eruptions can last several minutes, and intervals between eruptions can range from a few hours to several days.

The depressurized shaft of superheated water vaporizes into steam and shoots up into the air. **4**

When the water boils, some of it bubbles out above the surface. This causes a sudden drop in water pressure. **3**

2 More pressure builds when minerals dissolving from the surrounding rock are deposited on the walls of the underground conduit, constricting the opening.

Far below the surface, groundwater is heated in a confined space by the hot rocks surrounding it and by the pressure of the water itself. **1**

Sources: U.S. National Park Service (www.nps.gov) and U.S. Geological Survey (www.usgs.gov).

would probably never have become one of Iceland's favorite pastimes.

Iceland is also the only country in the world where the availability of electricity actually exceeds demand, so the use of high-temperature (240–310 degrees C.) water for generation of electricity has not been fully developed and much future potential remains. Water of this temperature tends to be high in minerals, and brackish if originating from fields near the sea, so it would form deposits that clog pipes if used directly. For this reason, it is used in cogeneration plants to generate electricity. Heat exchangers allow transfer heat to flow from mineral-laden water to pure water that is, in turn, used for heating and other low-temperature applications. At the same time, steam is separated from the source water to generate electricity. Waste brine

Its spa waters rich in minerals, Iceland's Blue Lagoon (shown here) is a popular tourist destination

from one such plant, at Swartsengi (pronounced SVART-sengi), in the southwest, fills a popular therapeutic pond called the Blue Lagoon.

Because heating is necessary almost year-round in Iceland, economics plays a big part in the technological development of energy sources there. Heating water is sold by meter to customers. According to Sverrir Thorhallsson, of Orkustofnun (pronounced ORK-oostopf-noon), the National Energy Authority of Iceland, "It is up to the user to extract as much heat from the water as possible to reduce the energy cost." Wastewater from district heating, still warm enough to melt snow, is piped under streets and parking lots throughout Reykjavik. Similar systems are being installed under driveways of private homes. Heat pumps are used in one district to extract heat from 35°C. return water to boost the temperature of another loop of return water, bringing what was once wastewater back to a reusable 80 degrees C.

Altogether, the efficient use of geothermal energy saves the people of Iceland a whopping $100 million (U.S.) in imported oil annually, and accounts for 49.5 percent of overall energy use in Iceland. Oil used to fuel cars and the nation's fishing fleet accounts for 30.5 percent of total energy consumption. The remaining 20 percent is provided from hydroelectricity.

Western States Are Increasing Their Use of Geothermal Energy

Alyssa Kagel and Karl Gawell

According to Alyssa Kagel and Karl Gawell, the western United States will require sixty thousand megawatts of new electric power by 2015. In response, many leading producers of geothermal energy are increasing production or building new geothermal power plants. So far, Arizona, California, Idaho, Nevada, and Utah have committed to more investment in geothermal energy. As geothermal energy has become more competitive with fossil fuels, companies are eager to expand geothermal production, they report. Kagel is outreach and research officer at the Geothermal Energy Association, and Gawell is executive director of the association.

After a period of stagnation, the geothermal industry is bursting with activity. Almost 500 megawatts [MW] of Power Purchase Agreements (PPA) were signed in just the first six months of 2005 for projects in Arizona, California, Idaho, Nevada and Utah. Many more projects are in the pipeline.

New data developed for the Geothermal Subcommittee of the Western Governors' Association (WGA) show 100 undeveloped geothermal power sites in the West, with a total power potential of 13,000 MW—enough to meet more than 70 percent of California's electricity needs.

Alyssa Kagel and Karl Gawell, "Geothermal Power on a Rebound," *Institutional Investor*, Vol. 39, December 2005, p.14. Reproduced by permission.

By 2015, 60,000 MW of new electric power will be needed in the West, the WGA estimates. The Governors want at least half of this to come from renewable and other clean energy technologies. With strong state Renewable Portfolio Standards in California, Nevada and other Western states, geothermal power is positioned for major expansion.

A More Competitive Industry

Congress has added its support by expanding the Production Tax Credit to include geothermal power. Now, geothermal power plants qualify for the same tax incentives as wind facilities—a 1.9 cent [per kilowatt-hour] credit for the first ten years of production—making geothermal power costs more competitive. At the opening of the newest geothermal plant in Nevada, Roberto Denis, Senior Vice President of Sierra Pacific Resources, said that geothermal power plants are producing power and selling it at rates that are competitive with their ability to generate it with fossil fuels, or buy it in the open wholesale market. He added, "The fossil fuel markets, gas, and coal have been going up significantly in prices. Having a stable source of energy that is stable in price is very important."

Besides favorable tax and regulatory environments, investments in geothermal projects have a number of other advantages. They are extremely reliable, with low costs over the lifetime of the plant, and a secure source of fuel. They provide power 24 hours a day, 365 days a year, with very minimal air and water impacts.

Geothermal is an environmentally preferred energy source, qualifying for green tags, renewable credits and similar attributes. As states, regions, and companies move ahead with plans to curb greenhouse gasses, carbon dioxide emissions are important to consider. Geothermal carbon dioxide emissions compare well with other renewables and are significantly lower than those from conventional fuels.

The performance of geothermal power matches the award winning nature of its leading companies. Ormat recently received the Distinguished Business of the Year Award from the Governor of Nevada. Calpine was recognized for the fourth

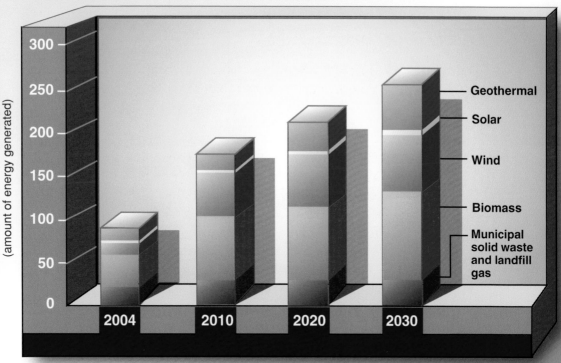

United States Renewable-Energy Generation
(Projected for Years 2004 to 2030)*

Kilowatt-Hours in Billions
(amount of energy generated)

300
250
200
150
100
50
0

2004   2010   2020   2030

Geothermal

Solar

Wind

Biomass

Municipal solid waste and landfill gas

*Hydroelectric power is not included in these future energy projections.
Source: U.S. Department of Energy, Energy Information Administration (www.eia.doe.gov), 2006.

consecutive year for their environmental and safety perform-ance by the California Department of Conservation.

Leading Producers and Developers

Calpine: is the largest producer of geothermal electricity from its facilities at The Geysers with a total capacity over 750 MW. In addition to new development at The Geysers, Calpine is also developing a project near the California-Oregon border. Calpine is included in the S&P [Standard and Poor's] 500 Index and is publicly traded on the New York Stock Exchange under the symbol CPN.

Caithness Energy: Caithness is one of the largest producers of renewable energy in the United States with geothermal facilities

A leading producer of geothermal energy, CalEnergy runs the geothermal power facility in the Salton Sea in California.

in California and Nevada totaling nearly 350 MW of capacity. Caithness continues to explore opportunities for acquiring and developing geothermal opportunities within the United States.

CalEnergy: CalEnergy's Salton Sea geothermal facilities produce 340 net MW. It has a contract to begin construction of a new 215 MW power plant, in late 2005 or early 2006. Additional commercial development of the estimated 2000 MW of available resource is also being examined. CalEnergy is a subsidiary of the MidAmerican Energy Holdings Corporation.

Ormat: Ormat operates geothermal facilities in Hawaii, Nevada and California with a total capacity of over 300 MW. Ormat, which recently placed in service a new geothermal plant in Nevada, is developing new production at its Ormesa and Heber Geothermal Complexes, and is pursuing development at new sites. Ormat Technologies, Inc., is traded on the New York Stock Exchange under the symbol ORA.

Amp Resources: Amp Resources is actively developing geothermal power projects throughout the world. Since 2002 Amp has acquired five development projects in the Western United States. They are actively pursuing additional project acquisitions and partnership opportunities.

Other geothermal companies developing new power projects include Vulcan Power and U.S. Geothermal.

Geothermal Production Can Benefit Communities

Geothermal Energy Association

According to the Geothermal Energy Association in this selection, geothermal energy provides economic and environmental benefits. Geothermal energy generates significant tax revenue and numerous new jobs in rural communities. For example, in Imperial County, California, the geothermal sector supplies $12 million in tax revenue and employs 285 people. Cities benefit as well. In Boise, Idaho, geothermal energy supplies heat to greenhouses, fish farms, and two hundred city buildings. Other communities gain from increased tourism, as when students, tourists, and scientists visit the Mammoth Lakes, California, geothermal power plant. The Geothermal Energy Association is a trade association composed of U.S. companies that support the expanded use of geothermal energy and are developing geothermal resources worldwide for electrical power generation and direct-heat uses.

What does the U.S. geothermal industry contribute to the economy? Geothermal energy provides low cost, reliable, environmentally friendly fuel; supplies thousands of quality jobs; boosts rural economies; increases tax bases; reduces foreign oil imports; stabilizes prices; and diversifies the fuel supply. A recent report indicates that 11,460 full time jobs were supported by the existing US geothermal industry in 2004. Unlike coal and natural gas, geothermal incurs no "hidden costs" such as land degradation, high air emissions, forced extinction and destruction of animals and plants, and health impacts to humans.

Helping Local Economies

What are some specific examples of ways in which geothermal energy has contributed to local economies?

Geothermal activities supply a full 25% of the county tax base in the rural town of Imperial County, California, producing over $12 million in tax revenue. In a town with a high rate of unemployment, the geothermal sector provides stable, well-paying jobs to over 285 people. CalEnergy, the largest geothermal company in the region, is the single largest taxpayer in Imperial County.

During a tour at a geothermal plant in New Mexico, a power plant official explains how a geothermal heat pump works.

Direct use applications installed in schools can provide huge savings to local communities. At four elementary schools in Lincoln, Nebraska where geothermal heat pumps have been installed, the heating and cooling savings total about $144,000 yearly, with total energy cost savings of 57%. Money provided from these savings are used to improve schools and revitalize communities.

Surrounded by natural beauty, this geothermal power plant located in Mammoth Lakes, California, is a tourist draw for the area.

Boise, Idaho highlights the variety of benefits that can be derived from geothermal direct use applications: the people of Idaho use geothermal resources to operate at least 15 greenhouses; geothermal aquaculture is popular: nine fish farms raise tilapia, catfish, alligators, and other fauna; an injection well for the city's geothermal heating system works to reduce discharge into the Boise river and replenish the geothermal aquifer the city shares with buildings; Boise's Capitol Mall, along with 200 other buildings, is heated by a geothermal system.

Future Benefits

Will new geothermal development contribute to local communities in the future?

Yes. Renewable Northwest Project reports that a 100 MW [megawatt] project in Eastern Oregon could create over a million dollars of additional local income each year, and would pay $4–6 million in local and state fees, royalties and taxes, even considering 1990 dollars (that have not been adjusted for inflation), according to the Oregon Department of Energy. In contrast, a similarly sized natural gas project sends $11–24 million out of the region every year for fuel costs alone.

According to a recent study, the construction of two new geothermal plants by Calpine Corporation in Siskiyou County, California will result in a total economic benefit of almost 114 million dollars over a thirty year period. This money will generate jobs, improve community living, and boost educational standards throughout the region.

Will geothermal energy influence tourism in my area?

Most geothermal power plants do not negatively affect tourism, and may even positively affect tourism. Take the example of the power plant at Mammoth Lakes, California, a site of skiing and mountain climbing, a land that one local described as Los Angeles' playground. Although people initially opposed the project due to worries over tourism impact, the project is now highly regarded among community members and visitors alike. Many people in the city do not even know the power plant exists because it was so expertly engineered to blend into the surrounding environment. The only example where tourism is affected occurs when students, scientists, or interested individuals visit the site of the power plant, thereby bringing business to the local community.

Rural Communities Stand to Benefit Most

What types of communities benefit most from geothermal development?
Most producible geothermal resources are located in rural areas. Rural communities tend to suffer from economic depression and high unemployment, and often contain large minority populations. A new plant ready to be built in California's Imperial Valley will bring a significant number of jobs to the Latino community there. Already, about 44 percent of the geothermal energy owner's employees are Latino. Besides providing a variety of jobs to individuals in these rural areas, geothermal developers are often the largest taxpayers in the communities in which they produce geothermal energy. The taxes generated by geothermal use can benefit local communities in the United States, with no money or jobs shipped overseas.

How much money does the geothermal industry contribute to the U.S. economy?
For every dollar invested on geothermal energy, the resulting growth of output to the U.S. economy is $2.50. This means that a geothermal investment of $280 million (e.g. a 100 MW power plant) would result in a growth of output of $700 million for the entire U.S. economy. This growth of output often benefits rural areas with high unemployment rates and significant minority communities. If 1000 megawatts of new geothermal power come online within the next three to five years as projected, the associated 2.8 billion dollar investment will result in a total economic output of $7 billion nationwide. In addition many geothermal firms develop geothermal projects overseas, and these technology export activities support the US economy and balance of trade.

No Hidden Costs

Are there any "hidden costs" associated with geothermal energy?
No. Hidden costs, including land degradation, dangerous air

A lone brown pelican skims the water for fish at a wildlife refuge near the Salton Sea geothermal power plant in California.

emissions, forced extinction and destruction of animals and plants, and health impacts to humans, are virtually nonexistent with geothermal energy production. In contrast, a 1995 study estimates that costs of power generation would increase 17 percent for natural gas and 25 percent for coal if hidden costs such as environmental impacts were included. Geothermal incurs none of these hidden costs because air emissions and other environmental impacts are minimal.

Lake County, California, downwind of The Geysers, the largest geothermal field under production in the world, is one of the only counties of California that has met all federal and state ambient air quality standards for seventeen years. At The Geysers, air quality has even improved as a result of geothermal development because hydrogen sulfide, which would ordinarily be released naturally into the atmosphere by geothermal features such as hot springs and fumaroles, instead now passes through an abatement system that reduces hydrogen sulfide emissions by 99.9 percent.

Instead of hidden costs, geothermal energy often has unrecognized benefits.

Facts About Geothermal Energy

Geothermal Definition

Geothermal refers to heat from the earth: *Geo* means earth; *therme* means heat.

Causes of Geothermal Activity

Geothermal energy is produced naturally by the heat generated inside Earth from decaying radioactive particles in rock. Nearly 4,000 miles beneath Earth's surface, the temperature of the heat generated in the planet's core ranges from about 5,000°F to 11,000°F (2760°C to 6100°C). Magma, or melted rock, rises to the surface where it can heat water in hot springs, cause geysers, or collect in volcanoes.

Sources of Geothermal Energy

Geysers, hot springs, volcanoes, fumaroles, and wells dug deep into the earth all supply geothermal energy.

Where Geothermal Resources Are Located

Geothermal resources are found along tectonic plate fractures in Earth's crust, typically in the Pacific Rim, the United States, Japan, Indonesia, the Philippines, and New Zealand. Such resources can also be found in Iceland, Africa, Russia, France, Italy, and coastal South America. In the United States geothermal activity appears primarily in the western states, including Arizona, California, Colorado, Idaho, Nevada, New Mexico, Oregon, Utah, and Hawaii.

Methods of Geothermal Energy Production

Flash Steam
- Hot water from the ground is converted into steam, which turns a turbine attached to a generator, which produces electricity.

Dry Steam
- Pressurized steam from a well is piped into a turbine attached to a generator, which produces electricity.

Binary Cycle
- A fluid is heated and its steam turns a turbine attached to a generator, which produces electricity. Then the steam is condensed into a liquid and injected back into the ground.

Hot Dry Rock
- Water is pumped into the earth to be warmed by geothermal activity and then brought to the surface where it becomes steam. The steam drives a turbine attached to a generator, which produces electricity.

Direct Uses for Geothermal Energy

Hot water over 50°F (10°C) and steam direct from the ground are used for agriculture, aquaculture, greenhouses, medicinal spas, heating buildings, and melting snow.

Energy Conversion

One megawatt, or 1 million watts, can supply adequate power to one thousand people.

Cost Effectiveness

Geothermal energy costs three to eight cents per kilowatt-hour (kWh) compared to four cents per kWh for coal.

Geothermal Energy Production Statistics

- As of 2003 geothermal energy was the third largest source of renewable energy in the United States, producing 2,800 megawatts.
- The United States produces the most geothermal energy in the world, generating an average of 15 billion kilowatt-hours annually.
- California is the state with the highest amount of electricity produced by geothermal resources, accounting for 5 percent of the state's electricity generation.

- Worldwide, 8,900 megawatts of geothermal energy supply 60 million people in twenty-four countries each year.

U.S. Geothermal Production Companies

- Calpine Corporation in San Jose, California (owns the majority of power plants at The Geysers geothermal field in northern California).
- CalEnergy Company in Omaha, Nebraska.
- Ormat International Inc. in Reno, Nevada.
- Unocal Corporation in El Segundo, California.
- U.S. Geothermal Inc. in Boise, Idaho.
- Vulcan Power Company in Bend, Oregon.

Research and Development

Numerous national laboratories are developing a better understanding of geothermal resources and production methods, such as innovations in exploration, advanced drilling technology, geothermal reservoir management, power plant performance, and geoscience advancements. Some of these laboratories include:

- Brookhaven National Laboratory
- Idaho National Engineering and Environmental Laboratory
- Lawrence Berkeley National Laboratory
- Lawrence Livermore National Laboratory
- National Renewable Energy Laboratory
- Sandia National Laboratories

Glossary

aquifer: A porous body of rock, sand, or gravel, that contains hot or cold water that can be tapped for wells or springs.

balneology: The science of baths that use therapeutic natural mineral water, such as in spas.

baseload power plant: A power plant that produces at least the minimum amount of electricity for a community continuously throughout the day, in contrast to peaker plants, which produce power only during peak usage times of the day.

binary cycle: A power-generating process that uses low-temperature geothermal hot water to heat another working fluid, usually an organic compound with a boiling point lower than water. This heated fluid then becomes steam, which turns a turbine attached to a generator to produce electricity. The steam is condensed back into a liquid and injected back into the ground to be reheated. Both the low-temperature water and working fluid are kept separate throughout the process.

combined cycle: A power-generating process that uses two methods, usually steam and binary cycle. At geothermal sites that provide both steam and hot water, the steam is pulled directly through the turbine to produce electricity, while the hot water is run through a binary cycle to produce even more electricity.

core: The hot interior of Earth. The outer core, which lies about 3,200 miles (5,100km) below the surface, is molten iron that surrounds a solid iron inner core about 4,000 miles (6,400km) below. Temperature of the core ranges from 7,200°F to 12,600°F (4,000°C to 7,000°C).

direct use: When hydrothermal, low-temperature water or steam is used as a direct source of energy rather than being directed through a power plant. Direct-use geothermal energy is used in agriculture, heating of public or private buildings, and at medicinal spas or hot springs.

dry steam: Steam from a geothermal well that is piped directly into a turbine to produce electricity. Condensed steam that has cooled into water is used as a cooling agent and some is reinjected back into the ground. The Geysers in California is a dry-steam power system.

dual-flash: A power-generating process that uses two flash-steam systems in a single plant. The plant pumps hot steam and lower-temperature steam into turbines to produce electricity.

dual-fuel system: A power system that uses geothermal energy as its main heating source and oil or natural gas as a supplement.

dual-well system: A power-generation system in which two boreholes are dug, one to withdraw hot water and the other to return the water back into the reservoir.

exploratory well: Holes drilled into the earth to determine the characteristics of a geothermal reservoir.

fault: A crack in Earth's crust. Movement of faults can cause earthquakes.

flash steam: A common power-generating process that pulls high-pressure hot water from the ground and flashes or converts it into steam, which is then used to drive a turbine to produce electricity. Leftover condensed steam and cooled water is then reinjected back into the reservoir.

fumarole: A hole or vent in Earth's crust through which steam and gases escape.

geopressured system: A geothermal deposit that contains sedimentary rocks and pressurized hot water, which has been trapped for eons. The water has been filtered through clay or shale and may contain natural gas.

geothermal: Describes heat that comes from the earth (from the Greek *geo* meaning "earth" and *therme* meaning "heat").

geothermal field: An area of land where natural and human-made geothermal activity is taking place.

geothermal gradient: The degree to which temperature increases with relation to depth in Earth's crust.

geothermal reserve: A natural collection of hot water below Earth's surface that is heated by magma.

gigawatt: A unit of electrical power equal to one thousand megawatts.

heat exchangers: A closed-loop system of pipes in which water or liquid such as isopentane or antifreeze is circulated throughout the system. The circulating liquid carries cold water into the ground to be heated in geothermal reservoirs and carries hot water up, usually into a building to heat it. Heat exchangers are popular for home heating.

hot dry rock: Geothermal hot rocks that heat water pumped through a borehole into the earth. The resulting hot water or steam is then pumped back to the surface where it is used to drive a turbine to generate electricity.

injection well: A well drilled into the earth consisting of a pipe through which geothermal water and energy production waste is returned to an underground reservoir. The pipe is cemented to the rock to prevent leakage and contamination of potable water.

kilowatt: A unit of electrical power equal to one thousand watts.

magma: Molten rock in Earth's mantle that reaches the surface through fissures or volcanoes.

mantle: The 1,800-mile- (2,900km)-thick layer between Earth's outer crust and interior core.

megawatt: A unit of electrical power equal to 1 million watts.

plates: The layer of Earth's crust that is separated into pieces called plates. These tectonic plates move around the globe in what is called the continental drift.

renewable: An energy source that is continually replenished or recharged and is never depleted.

Ring of Fire: A ring of countries and continents surrounding the Pacific Ocean where plate-tectonic and geothermal activity is common. The Ring of Fire includes Japan, the Philippines, the Aleutian Islands, North America, Central America, and South America.

scrubber: Chemical filtering equipment that removes potentially harmful gases from power plant emissions before they are released into the air. Geothermal plants use scrubbers to filter out hydrogen sulfide and other gases.

sludge: The solid material that remains after the scrubbing process. Sludge can contain useful materials like zinc and sulfur that can be resold; and it can produce harmful materials like arsenic, chloride, and mercury, which present waste disposal problems.

sustainable energy: Energy that can be continually generated and consumed to meet the needs of a community for several generations.

Chronology

Ca. 10,000 B.C.
Throughout the ancient world, Native Americans, Greeks, Romans, Chinese, and Japanese use naturally occurring hot springs for cooking, heating, bathing, and healing.

A.D. 1326
The first health spa opens in Belgium. It is called Espa, meaning fountain, and uses natural hot springs.

1755
Eggert Olafsson and Bjarni Palsson dig the first wells to tap into hot springs in Reykjavik, Iceland.

1830
In the first documented commercial use of geothermal energy in the United States, Asa Thompson charges a dollar for baths in a tub filled with water fed by natural hot springs.

1847
Surveyor William Bell Elliott finds hot springs and fumaroles north of San Francisco, California, which he names The Geysers. He tells friends the site is like "the Gates of Hell."

1852
The Geysers Resort Hotel and spa opens. Over the years the hotel hosts Ulysses S. Grant, Theodore Roosevelt, and Mark Twain.

1890
The first exploratory geothermal well in the United States is drilled near Boise, Idaho.

1892
The town of Warm Springs, Idaho, pipes hot water from geothermal wells into town buildings, thereby establishing the first district heating system from a geothermal source. The Boise

Natatorium, a recreational building housing a geothermally heated swimming pool, opens.

1904

Prince Piero Ginori Conti in Italy invents the first electric generator powered by geothermal steam; this technology is installed at the Larderello hot springs in Tuscany to become the world's first electric power plant to run on geothermal energy.

1922

John D. Grant builds America's first geothermal power plant at The Geysers. The plant eventually generates 250 kilowatts of electricity, which lights the resort's buildings and streets. Soon, however, the pipes corrode and the plant becomes uncompetitive with other energy plants.

1923

The first direct-cycle power plant, which is fed with natural steam directly from a well, is installed at Serrazano, Italy.

1925

The first experimental geothermal power plant in Japan is built in Beppu, Kyushu.

1927

At the Salton Sea in Southern California, Pioneer Development Company drills geothermal exploration wells to search for a natural source of steam to generate power for the area.

1930

The first commercial use of geothermal energy to heat a greenhouse in the United States is in Edward's Greenhouses in Boise, Idaho. In November, in Iceland, hot water is piped three kilometers from a well to a school in Reykjavik; the school is the first building in Iceland to be heated by geothermal energy.

1948

Professor Carl Nielsen of Ohio State University builds the first ground-source heat pump for residential use; commercial use of the technology follows soon after.

1955

The U.S. geothermal industry is officially launched when B.C.

McCabe founds the Magma Power Company, an outfit that drills the first modern geothermal well and opens steam developing operations at The Geysers.

1958
The first geothermal power plant to utilize the wet steam process goes on line in the volcanic Wairakei Valley on New Zealand's North Island. In October the first modern commercial contract for purchasing geothermal electrical power is drafted when Pacific Gas and Electric Company in California buys steam from Magma-Thermal.

1960
The first power plant in the United States to generate electricity from geothermal steam goes on line at The Geysers; operated by Pacific Gas and Electric, the plant produces eleven megawatts of power.

1966
Japan's first full-scale commercial power plant comes on line at Matsukawa Geothermal Power Station on the island of Honshu.

1967
Union Oil Company (Unocal) in California begins commercial development of The Geysers steam fields.

1970
The Geothermal Resources Council is established to encourage the development of geothermal resources and to disseminate information worldwide, and the U.S. Geothermal Steam Act authorizes the Secretary of the Interior to lease land for development of geothermal resources.

1972
The Geothermal Energy Association is established as a trade association composed of U.S. companies that promote the use of geothermal energy worldwide.

1973
The Philippine National Oil Company contracts with Unocal to exploit the Tiwi and Makiling-Banahaw geothermal fields in

the Philippines; three years later the Philippines begins its first electric power generation from geothermal energy. The first geothermal power plant in Mexico comes on line at the Cierro Prieto in Chihuahua.

1973

The House Science and Astronautics Committee sponsors a bill that directs the National Science Foundation to fund research in geothermal energy and directs the National Aeronautics and Space Administration to demonstrate technologies for commercial use of geothermal resources.

1974

The Geothermal Energy Research, Development, and Demonstration Act (RD&D) is enacted to give the U.S. Geological Society responsibility for evaluating and assessing geothermal resources. The Energy Research and Development Administration replaces the Atomic Energy Commission in order to increase the U.S. federal government's research and development of alternative forms of energy. The Division of Geothermal Energy takes over the RD&D program.

1975

The Geo-Heat Center is created to disseminate information on multipurpose uses of geothermal energy. The U.S. Geological Survey releases "Assessment of Geothermal Resources in the United States," the first report to establish the methodology for geothermal resource assessments and to provide estimates of potential electric power generation.

1977

The newly formed U.S. Department of Energy (DOE) takes over most of the government's energy programs. The Geothermal Technologies Program falls under the DOE's Office of Energy Efficiency and Renewable Energy.

1978

Congress enacts the U.S. Public Utility Regulatory Policies Act. To encourage energy efficiency, the law requires electric utilities to purchase electricity from small power producers who use renewable energy, such as geothermal power.

1980

The Geysers Resort in California is razed, ending much of the tourism to the area.

1982

By 1982 geothermal electricity-generating capacity has reached a high of one thousand megawatts.

1988

The nonprofit, nongovernmental International Geothermal Association, based in Iceland, is established to promote education and encourage research and development of geothermal resources worldwide. In the United States electricity production at The Geysers peaks at roughly two thousand megawatts. Reduced steam pressure at the field eventually causes production to decline.

1990

The U.S. Department of Energy's funding for geothermal energy research and development reaches a low of $15 million.

1991

The first magma exploratory well is drilled at the Long Valley Exploratory Well near Mammoth Lakes, California; magma was not found inside the caldera.

1994

After acquiring Magma Power Corporation and projects in the Philippines, California Energy Company becomes the world's largest geothermal company.

1995

Worldwide geothermal capacity reaches six thousand megawatts.

2000

The DOE creates the GeoPowering the West initiative, which funds public and private partnerships to develop new technologies and explore geothermal resources in the western United States.

2001

Passage of the Securing America's Future Energy Act, which amends the Geothermal Steam Act of 1970, aims to promote energy conservation through creation of tax credits for the use and development of energy-efficient technologies.

2003

At the International Geothermal Conference in Reykjavik, Iceland, the Beijing Municipal Government announces its plan to utilize geothermal energy for space heating and hot water for facilities that will be used for the 2008 Summer Olympic Games.

2005

The $1.5 billion per year U.S. geothermal industry produces more than twenty-eight hundred megawatts of electricity and two thousand megawatts of thermal energy for direct-use applications.

2006

The "Fiscal Year 2007 Budget-in-Brief" of the Energy Efficiency and Renewable Energy office calls for the elimination of funding for the Geothermal Technologies Program, including the Geo-Powering the West Program, as of fiscal 2007. In contradiction, the Energy Policy Act of 2005 raises funding to $32.5 million for 2007 for the Geothermal Technologies Program.

For Further Reading

Books and Papers

Conn Abnee, "Renewable Fuels," Geothermal Heat Pump Consortium, July 24, 2001. www.eere.energy.gov.

Paula Berinstein, *Alternative Energy: Facts, Statistics, and Issues.* Westport, CT: Oryx, 2001.

P.M. Boekhoff and Stuart A. Kallen, *Geysers.* San Diego: Kidhaven, 2003.

Robert K. Dixon, "Geothermal Resources on Public Lands," U.S. Department of Energy. May 3, 2001. www.doe.gov.

Wendell A. Duffield, *Geothermal Energy: Clean Power from the Earth's Heat.* Menlo Park, CA: U.S. Geological Survey, 2003.

Sandra Friend, *Earth's Fiery Fury.* Brookfield, CT: Twenty-First Century, 2000.

Karl Gawell, "Enhancing Energy Security," Geothermal Energy Association, March 19, 2003. www.eere.energy.gov.

———, "The Future of Geothermal Energy." Geothermal Energy Association, July 22, 2003. www.eere.energy.gov.

Ian Graham, *Geothermal and Bio-Energy.* Austin, TX: Raintree Steck-Vaughn, 1999.

Gabriel Gruden, *Energy Alternatives.* Detroit: Lucent, 2005.

Margaret Hall, *Yellowstone National Park.* Chicago: Heinemann Library, 2006.

Claire Llewellyn, *Geysers*. Chicago: Heinemann Library, 2000.

Sally Morgan, *Alternative Energy Sources*. Chicago: Heinemann Library, 2003.

Christine Petersen, *Alternative Energy: A True Book*. New York: Children's, 2004.

Richard Plunz et al., *Geothermal Larderello: Tuscany, Italy*. New York: Princeton Architectural Press, 2005.

Julie Richards, *Geothermal Energy and Bio-Energy*. North Mankato, MN: Smart Apple Media, 2004.

Peter F. Smith, *Sustainability at the Cutting Edge: Emerging Technologies for Low Energy Buildings*. Oxford, MA: Architectural Press, 2003.

U.S. Department of Energy, *Geothermal Energy Program Highlights*. Golden, CO: National Renewable Energy Laboratory, 1999.

Jonathan Weisgall, "Alternative Energy Sources on Public Lands." Geothermal Energy Association, October 3, 2001. www.eere.energy.gov.

Periodicals and Internet Sources

W.T. Box Jr. and Charlene Wardlow, "A Second Boom for Geothermal," *Power Engineering*, June 2004.

Chris Bramley, "Geothermal Future," *Geographical*, July 2003.

California Energy Commission, "Energy Story: Chapter 11: Geothermal Energy," April 22, 2002. www.energyquest.ca.gov.

Roberto Carella, "Survey of Energy Resources: Geothermal Energy," European Geothermal Energy Council, World Energy Council, 2001. www.worldenergy.org.

Emma Davy, "Pipe Dream," *Current Science*, February 22, 2005.

Harald Franzen, "A Church Digs Deep," *Popular Science*, April 2002.

Ingvar B. Fridleifsson, "Geothermal Energy for the Benefit of the People." United Nations University, Geothermal Training Programme, 2001. http://iga.igg.cnr.it.

Tyler Hamilton, "Geothermal Targets Mainstream Down to Earth," *Toronto Star*, April 24, 2006.

Barbara Horwitz-Bennett, "Below the Surface," *Consulting-Specifying Engineer*, March 2004.

J.B. Hulen and P.M. Wright, "Geothermal Energy, Clean Sustainable Energy for the Benefit of Humanity and the Environment," Energy and Geoscience Institute, May 2001. www.geothermal.org.

Julie V. Iovine, "Old Heating Idea Heats Up," *New York Times*, January 4, 2001.

Jeff Israely, "Steaming Forward," *Time Europe*, June 16, 2003.

Peter Janssen, "The Too-Slow Flow," *Newsweek*, September 20, 2004.

Junona Jonas, "Primer on Geothermal Energy," *Electric Light & Power*, November 2003.

Alyssa Kagel and Karl Gawell, "Geothermal Power on a Rebound," *Institutional Investor*, December 2005.

Alyssa Kagel, Diana Bates, and Karl Gawell, "A Guide to Geothermal Energy and the Environment," Geothermal Energy Association, April 22, 2005. www.geo-energy.org.

Laboratory of Energy, Ecology, and Economy, University of

Applied Sciences of Southern Switzerland, "Energy: The Future Is Geothermal," November 2005. www.ticinoricerca.ch.

Naomi Lubick, "California Heats Up over Natural Steam," *Scientific American*, December 10, 2001.

John W. Lund, "100 Years of Geothermal Power Generation," Geo-Heat Center, September 2004. http://geoheat.oit.edu.

Carol Lynn MacGregor, "Pioneer Geothermal Development in Boise, Idaho," *Journal of the West*, January 1999.

Dean E. Murphy, "U.S. Approves Power Plant in Area Indians Hold Sacred," *New York Times*, November 28, 2002.

National Renewable Energy Laboratory, "Careers in Renewable Energy," Energy Efficiency and Renewable Energy Clearinghouse, 2001. www.nrel.gov.

Zena Olijnyk, "Full Steam Ahead," *Canadian Business*, September 12, 2005.

Fred Pearce, "East Africa Eyes Up Hot Rocks for Fuel of the Future," *New Scientist*, May 3, 2003.

————, "Underground Power Hots Up," *New Scientist*, April 3, 2004.

Jeff Persons, "The Big Dig," *Mother Earth News*, May 2001.

Jay Romano, "Geothermal Heating Systems," *New York Times*, December 22, 2002.

Vicky Sanderson, "Energy Alternatives Gaining Popularity," *Toronto Star*, March 4, 2006.

Jon Swan, "Fire and Ice," *Amicus Journal*, Winter 2000.

————, "The Icelandic Rift," *Orion*, March/April 2004.

Lyn Topinka, "The Plus Side of Volcanoes: Geothermal Energy," Cascades Volcano Observatory, U.S. Geological Survey, January 3, 2006. http://vulcan.wr.usgs.gov.

Jessica Worden, "Clean Heat," *E Magazine: The Environmental Magazine*, January/February 2005.

Web Sites

California Energy Commission (www.energy.ca.gov). Formed in 1981, the commission's Geothermal Program promotes geothermal energy development in California and provides financial assistance to private entities for research, development, and commercialization projects. The Web site offers fact sheets on projects funded, a list of resource assessment projects, a map of California's geothermal areas, and an overview of geothermal energy in the state.

Energy Efficiency and Renewable Energy (www.eere.energy.gov). Part of the U.S. Department of Energy, the Energy Efficiency and Renewable Energy's Geothermal Technologies Program works with industry to establish geothermal energy as an economically competitive contributor to the U.S. energy supply. The Web site offers a history of geothermal energy, photos, research and development, educational resources, a calendar of events, and a list of associations.

Geothermal Education Office (http://geothermal.marin.org). Funded by the U.S. Department of Energy and the geothermal industry, the education office promotes public understanding about geothermal resources and distributes educational material about geothermal energy to schools, libraries, industry, and the public. The Web site contains geothermal facts, an educational slide show, classroom materials, a glossary, and links to other Web sites.

Geothermal Energy Association (www.geo-energy.org). The Geothermal Energy Association is a U.S. trade group that encourages research to improve geothermal technologies, develops geothermal resources worldwide for electrical power generation and direct-heat uses, and provides a forum for discussion of geothermal issues. The Web site provides an explanation of geothermal energy, literature, and trade show information.

Geothermal Resources Council (www.geothermal.org). The council is an association of geothermal professionals and companies from around the world that promotes development, outreach, information, and technology transfer among its members. The Web site presents information on the U.S. Department of Energy Geothermal Technologies Programs, publications, workshops, a calendar of events, and notice of annual meetings.

International Geothermal Association (http://iga.igg.cnr.it). Founded in 1988, the IGA is a nonpolitical, scientific, educational, and cultural organization that encourages research and development of geothermal resources worldwide. The Web site explains the fundamentals of geothermal energy, presents statistics of worldwide development and use of geothermal energy, and offers publications from conferences.

National Geothermal Collaborative (www.geocollaborative. org). Formed in 2002, the collaborative gathers representatives from utilities, developers, sustainable energy advocates, and state and federal government sectors for the purpose of developing efficient and environmentally sound use of geothermal resources. The Web site describes the group's objectives, protocols and guidelines, activities, and steering committees.

National Renewable Energy Lab (www.nrel.gov). Begun in 1974, the research and development lab is now part of the U.S. Department of Energy. Its mission is to secure an energy future for the nation that is environmentally and economically sustainable.

Renewable Energy Policy Project (www.crest.org). The Renewable Energy Policy Project supports the advancement of renewable energy technology through policy analysis, innovative strategies, and information dissemination. The Geothermal Energy page contains information on geothermal resources, history, technology, economics, environmental impacts, policy, and future developments.

Index

energy
  research on conservation of,
    64
  sources of, 51
Energy Bill (2005), 71–72,
  74-75
Energy Efficiency and
  Renewable Energy Office
  (EERE), 42
Energy Policy Act (1992), 14
Energy Research and
  Development
  Administration, 12
environment
  geothermal energy benefits,
    48, 95, 99
  renewable energy harms,
    52–53

Fell, Nolan, 76
"Field Verification of Small-
  Scale Geothermal Power
  Plants" (Department of
  Energy), 67
flash steam power plants, 28,
  45
Flavin, Christopher, 56
fossil fuels
  geothermal and, 67
  renewable energy and, 50
Frey, Norman, 72

Gaschnitz, Roland, 79, 80
Gawell, Karl, 40, 89

geopressured deposits, 22
"Geothermal Electric Power
  Production in the United
  States" (report), 66–67
geothermal energy
  challenges for, 37–38
  companies developing,
    90–93
  direct use applications of,
    36–37
  forms of, 22–23
  has no hidden costs, 95, 99
  historical use of, 19, 21
  in Iceland, 83
  incentives for development
    of, 62, 74
  industrial applications of,
    30, 31
  is not renewable, 56–57
  nations using, 39
  oil prices and development
    of, 10
  potential of, 31–32, 64–65
  problems with, 13–14,
    54–56
  research on
    by Energy Department,
      63–64
    government spending for,
      11–12
    oil prices and, 14
  sold byproducts of, 46–47,
    66
  sources of, 20

Picture Credits

About the Editor

Lorraine Savage received a B.A. in writing from Roger Williams University in Bristol, Rhode Island. She was an assistant editor at H.W. Wilson Company, editing *Wilson Business Abstracts*, and an associate editor at the PennWell Corporation, where she edited the publication *Solid State Technology* and wrote for *Computer Graphics World*. She has also served as managing editor at *Healthcare Review*. Savage has written for Thomson Gale since 1999 for such publications as *Biography Resource Center*, *Contemporary Theatre*, *Film and Television*, *Encyclopedia of World Biographies*, *International Directory of Business Biographies*, *Mathematics for Students*, and *Notable Sports Figures*. *Geothermal Power* is the first book she has edited for Greenhaven Press. Her other writing interests include Japanese culture and pets and animal care.

GRA 741.5 BAT V.5
Pak, Greg,
Batman/Superman. Truth hurts /

VOLUME 5
TRUTH HURTS

BATMAN/SUPERMAN

VOLUME 5
TRUTH HURTS

BATMAN/SUPERMAN

WRITTEN BY
GREG PAK

PENCILS BY
ARDIAN SYAF
CLIFF RICHARDS
YILDIRAY CINAR
HOWARD PORTER
JACK HERBERT

INKS BY
VICENTE CIFUENTES
CLIFF RICHARDS
YILDIRAY CINAR
HOWARD PORTER
JACK HERBERT

COLOR BY
BETH SOTELO
ULISES ARREOLA
DEAN WHITE
WIL QUINTANA
BLOND

LETTERS BY
ROB LEIGH

COLLECTION COVER BY
ARDIAN SYAF
DANNY MIKI
ULISES ARREOLA

SUPERMAN CREATED BY
JERRY SIEGEL & JOE SHUSTER
BY SPECIAL ARRANGEMENT WITH
THE JERRY SIEGEL FAMILY

BATMAN CREATED BY
BOB KANE
WITH **BILL FINGER**

ANDREW MARINO JEREMY BENT Assistant Editors – Original Series
EDDIE BERGANZA Group Editor – Original Series
JEB WOODARD Group Editor – Collected Editions
SUZANNAH ROWNTREE Editor – Collected Edition
STEVE COOK Design Director – Books
DAMIAN RYLAND Publication Design

BOB HARRAS Senior VP – Editor-in-Chief, DC Comics

DIANE NELSON President
DAN DIDIO and JIM LEE Co-Publishers
GEOFF JOHNS Chief Creative Officer
AMIT DESAI Senior VP – Marketing & Global Franchise Management
NAIRI GARDINER Senior VP – Finance
SAM ADES VP – Digital Marketing
BOBBIE CHASE VP – Talent Development
MARK CHIARELLO Senior VP – Art, Design & Collected Editions
JOHN CUNNINGHAM VP – Content Strategy
ANNE DEPIES VP – Strategy Planning & Reporting
DON FALLETTI VP – Manufacturing Operations
LAWRENCE GANEM VP – Editorial Administration & Talent Relations
ALISON GILL Senior VP – Manufacturing & Operations
HANK KANALZ Senior VP – Editorial Strategy & Administration
JAY KOGAN VP – Legal Affairs
DEREK MADDALENA Senior VP – Sales & Business Development
JACK MAHAN VP – Business Affairs
DAN MIRON VP – Sales Planning & Trade Development
NICK NAPOLITANO VP – Manufacturing Administration
CAROL ROEDER VP – Marketing
EDDIE SCANNELL VP – Mass Account & Digital Sales
COURTNEY SIMMONS Senior VP – Publicity & Communications
JIM (SKI) SOKOLOWSKI VP – Comic Book Specialty & Newsstand Sales
SANDY YI Senior VP – Global Franchise Management

BATMAN/SUPERMAN VOLUME 5: TRUTH HURTS

DC Comics, 2900 West Alameda Ave., Burbank, CA 91505
Printed by RR Donnelley, Salem, VA. 7/8/16. First Printing.
ISBN: 978-1-4012-6369-0

Library of Congress Cataloging-in-Publication Data is available.

AW DAD'S
ACTOR RUN
R A *RABBIT*
HEN I WAS
FOUR.

AAAAA!

IT *SCREAMED*
JUST LIKE THAT.

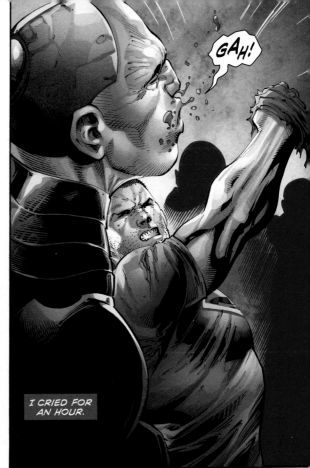

GAH!

I *CRIED* FOR
AN HOUR.

AAAGH!

LONG TIME
AGO.

NEVER *PUNCH*
DOWN, MY FATHER
ALWAYS SAID.

BUT
I *SWEAR,*
POP...

RANCH

WE GOT ORDERS.

ORDERS?

THEY SAID YOU *LOST* YOUR *POWERS.*

YOU SHOULDN'T BE ON THE STREETS.

YOU'RE JUST A *MAGNET* FOR THESE *MANIACS.*

BRINGING TROUBLE ON YOURSELF.

AND THE REST OF THE CITY.

THEY SAY LET YOU *REAP* WHAT YOU *SOW.*

"THEY," *huh?*

WE GET *MEMOS.* I DON'T KNOW WHERE THE ORDERS COME FROM.

I MIGHT.

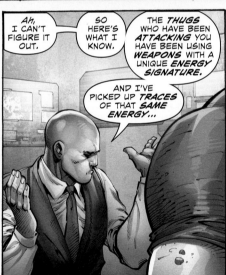

Ah, I CAN'T FIGURE IT OUT.

SO HERE'S WHAT I KNOW.

THE *THUGS* WHO HAVE BEEN *ATTACKING* YOU HAVE BEEN USING *WEAPONS* WITH A UNIQUE *ENERGY SIGNATURE.*

AND I'VE PICKED UP *TRACES* OF THAT *SAME ENERGY...*

...IN *GOTHAM CITY.*

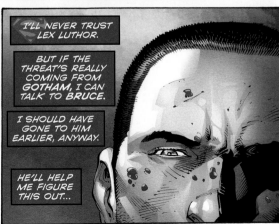

I'LL NEVER TRUST LEX LUTHOR.

BUT IF THE THREAT'S REALLY COMING FROM GOTHAM, I CAN TALK TO BRUCE.

I SHOULD HAVE GONE TO HIM EARLIER, ANYWAY.

HE'LL HELP ME FIGURE THIS OUT...

...SAPPEARING IN THE MIDDLE OF A CONVERSATION.

HE'S STEALING YOUR SCHTICK, BATMAN.

IF HE'S REALLY WORKING FOR YOU, YOU'D BETTER START EXPLAINING THINGS.

HOW DID THIS MESS START, ANYWAY?

DOUBTFUL. DID MR. KENT ATTACK YOU, GENTLEMEN?

NO, SIR.

THERE WERE THESE... BARBARIANS. IN SPACE ARMOR.

HE WAS BREAKING INTO THE WAYNETECH BUILDING.

AND KENT SAVED YOU.

YEAH.

AND THESE SPACE BARBARIANS GOT AWAY WHEN BATMAN ATTACKED.

Uh.

YEAH.

SUPERMAN'S BEEN STALKED BY VARIOUS THUGS CARRYING STRANGE WEAPONS.

I HELPED HIM TRACK THE ENERGY SIGNATURE HERE TO GOTHAM.

I'M NOT PICKING UP ANYTHING STRANGE.

OF COURSE, YOU IDIOT...

...SUPERMAN TOOK THE EVIDENCE.

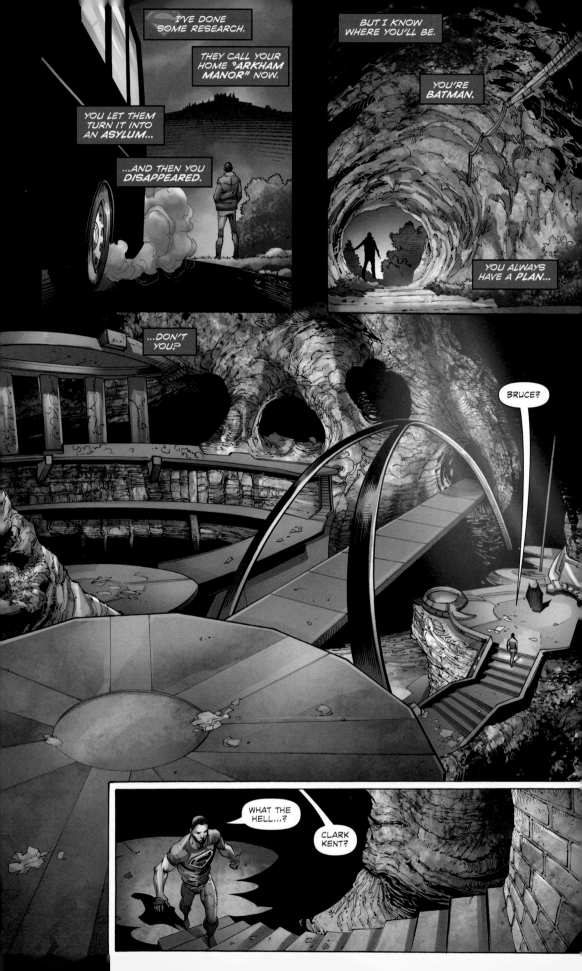

ALFRED!

Ah! APOLOGIES FOR... *SURPRISING* YOU.

I DIDN'T ACTUALLY REALIZE THAT WAS POSSIBLE.

YEAH, WELL.

THINGS HAVE CHANGED.

THEY CERTAINLY HAVE.

WHERE'S BRUCE?

MAYBE I CAN HELP YOU. THIS IS THE PROBLEM, eh?

ALFRED...

INTERESTING. I'M GUESSING YOU NEED AN ANALYSIS...

I DON'T HAVE THE *SUPER-HEARING* TO READ HIS *HEARTBEAT*...

ALFRED.

...OR THE *SUPER-SIGHT* TO COUNT THE MOLECULES OF *EPINEPHRINE* IN HIS BLOODSTREAM...

...BUT I CAN STILL TELL WHEN A FRIEND IS... *GRIEVING*.

...JUST TALK TO ME.

...ALFRED WAS TRAINED AS AN ACTOR.

WHERE ARE YOU REALLY, BRUCE?

A MONTH AGO, I COULD HAVE FOUND YOU IN SECONDS, ANYWHERE IN THE WORLD, JUST BY LISTENING FOR YOUR HEARTBEAT.

NOW I WOULDN'T KNOW IF YOU WERE ACROSS THE STREET.

BUT IF YOU'RE ALIVE...

...YOU HAVE TO KNOW I'M HERE, DON'T YOU?

YOU ALWAYS KNOW EVERYTHING.

SO WHY DON'T YOU CALL?

DAMMIT.

HELLO?

HEY.

...CLARK?

HEY. LOIS.

LONG TIME NO TALK.

YYYEAH...

...HOW ARE YOU?

GOOD.

GOOD.

...

...

GENERALLY THE PERSON WHO *CALLS* INITIATES THE *CONVERSATION.*

SORRY. OKAY. I'M IN *GOTHAM*...

I KNOW.

YOU KNOW?

I HEARD THE *WHISTLE* OF THE EAST SIDE *EL.*

AND YOU WERE KIND OF ALL OVER THE *NEWS* LAST NIGHT.

FIGHTING WITH BATMAN

YOU'RE IN TROUBLE, AREN'T YOU?

WELL, OF COURSE I'M IN TROUBLE.

SOMEONE TOLD THE *WORLD* ABOUT MY *SECRET IDENTITY.*

OKAY. THIS *AGAIN*?

WE'VE BEEN OVER THIS. YOU KNOW WHY I DID IT.

AND *DIANA* KNOWS. DIDN'T SHE TELL YOU--

Nngh.

DON'T YOU *GRUNT* AT ME, CLARK KENT.

NO, WAIT. THAT CAME OUT WRONG.

Tch. I'M NOT TRYING TO--

LOOK, I'M NOT *RIGHT* EVERY TIME, CLARK.

BUT NEITHER ARE *YOU.*

AND IT HASN'T BEEN PARTICULARLY *AWESOME* OVER HERE, EITHER, YOU KNOW.

YOU'RE RIGHT, LOIS.

AND YOU'RE RIGHT, TOO, ALFRED.

I'M NOT BUILT TO LIVE LIKE THIS.

IN DARKNESS AND SUSPICION.

I BELONG IN THE SUN.

IF WE DON'T WORK TOGETHER...

...PEOPLE ARE GONNA DIE.

HEY!

WHOEVER'S DOING THIS DOESN'T WANT A SUPERMAN AROUND TO SAVE THE DAY.

OR A BATMAN, I'M GUESSING.

YOU'RE HIDING YOUR FACE. SO I KNOW YOU FEAR THE CONSEQUENCES OF WHAT YOU DO.

THEY'LL COME FOR YOU, JUST LIKE THEY CAME FOR ME.

YOU CAN FACE THEM ALL ALONE.

AND RISK EVERYONE YOU'RE SUPPOSEDLY PROTECTING.

OR YOU CAN HAVE SUPERMAN BACKING YOU UP.

HELL, YOU KNOW WHAT?

LET'S STOP PRETENDING YOU'VE GOT A CHOICE.

I'M RIDING THIS TO THE END.

SO YOU'RE GONNA HAVE TO DEAL WITH ME NO MATTER WHAT.

BUT I GOTTA TELL YA...

...THE REAL BATMAN'S GOT MUCH COOLER TOYS THAN THAT.

Psh.

SO NOW YOU'RE TRYING TO MOVE IT?

YES. WE'RE NEARLY DONE ASSEMBLING THE SHIELDING--

PROPERLY DEVELOPED, IT COULD POWER THE *ENTIRE COUNTRY* FOR A *HUNDRED YEARS.*

BUT AT THIS STAGE, ANY ATTEMPT TO TAP IT COULD CAUSE IT TO *DETONATE...*

...AND YES, *KILL EVERYONE* WITHIN *THREE MILES.*

ALL RIGHT, YOU HELP 'EM WRAP UP HERE.

I'M GONNA GO GREET THE *DAWN.*

WHAT THE--

CLANK

PAY MORE ATTENTION, BUDDY.

YOU'RE *STRONG,* BUT YOU'RE *SLOW.*

I'LL HOLD OFF WHATEVER'S COMING UNTIL--

YOU'RE NOT GOING ANYWHERE--

RRRUMMMBBLLE

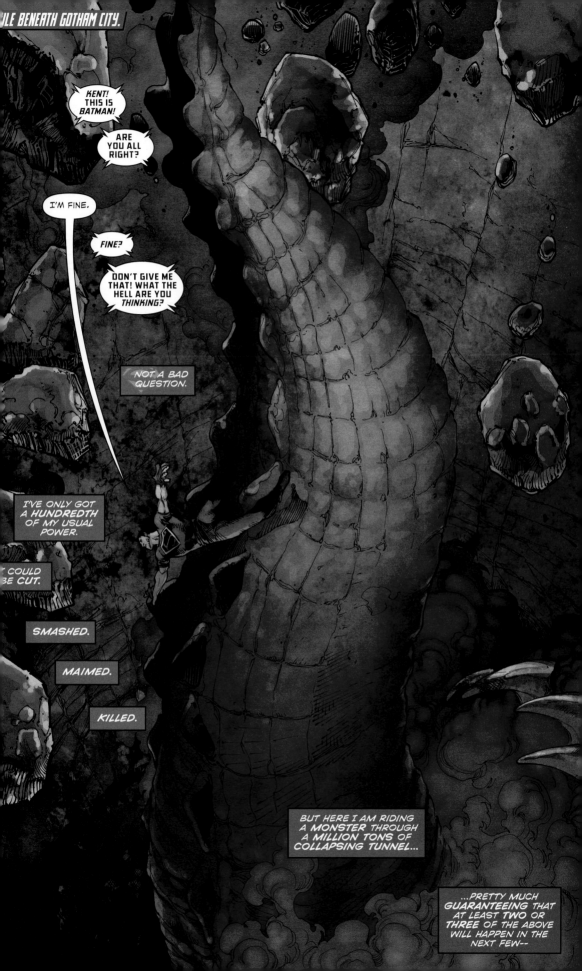

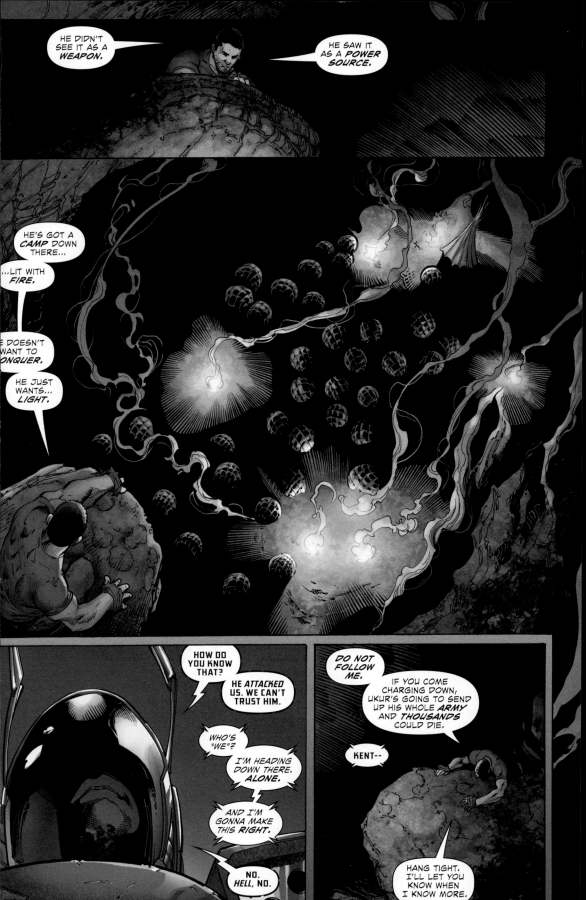

IN DISGUISE.

PROWLING THROUGH THE SHADOWS.

STEALING YOUR SCHTICK AGAIN, BRUCE.

BUT IT FEELS GOOD.

AND THAT FEELS STRANGE.

I'VE GOT A SECRET IDENTITY AGAIN.

AND AFTER LOSING THE FORTRESS... SMALLVILLE... METROPOLIS...

...AND SO MANY FRIENDS...

...I'M ALMOST EMBARRASSED BY HOW A COSTUME CAN MAKE ME ALMOST FEEL--

--SAFE--

GRRRAAAAA!

HEY, NOW!

AGH. THINKING LIKE THE OLD ME.

COULD HAVE GOTTEN MY ARM BITTEN OFF--

AAAAAAAGH!

WHA--

AAAAAGH!

RUN!

I KNOW A SUBTERRANEAN CHILD WHO COULD KNOCK ONE OF THESE MONSTERS OUT WITH A SINGLE PUNCH.

BUT THESE FOLKS ARE JUST HUMAN...

HYAAA!

...KINDA LIKE ME.

DAMMIT, UKUR.

I WAS TRYING TO SNEAK IN QUIETLY...

ROBBIE!

MOMMY!

OH, MY GOD, BABY...

THANKS, FELLA!

EVERYONE... EVERYONE OKAY?

YEAH, YEAH. THE BULLS'RE NORMALLY REAL GOOD, BUT THEY BOLTED WHEN THE ROOF STARTED FALLING IN.

SO WHAT...YOU'RE ONE OF THE *DAWN COMMAND*?

AH, YEAH.

AND WHO ARE *YOU*?

YOU AND YOUR CREW DON'T LOOK LIKE *SUBTERRANEANS*.

OH, YEAH. WE'RE HUMAN. "UPPERWORLDERS," THEY CALL US.

GOTHAM?

YEAH. THERE WAS SOME CRAZY BATMAN THING GOING ON A WHILE BACK.

GOTHAM PRISON.

EXPLOSIONS, FIRE IN THE SKY, ALL THAT. AND THE PRISON KIND OF CRACKED UP AND A BUNCH OF US...

...WELL, WE DECIDED OUR TIME WITH THE INSTITUTION HAD COME TO A NATURAL CONCLUSION.

ONE OF THE CRACKS LED TO THE TUNNELS UNDER THE CITY.

AND THAT'S WHERE WE FOUND *UKUR*.

TRADED ONE PRISON FOR ANOTHER, *huh*?

WHAT? NO!

WE JOINED UP.

THAT THE LAST OF IT?

UNTIL YOU FEED 'EM AGAIN, I'M GUESSING.

HA. WELL, YOU AIN'T TOO GOOD TO GET INTO IT, ANYWAY.

I GREW UP ON A FARM...

...SHOVELED A LOTTA DUNG IN MY DAY.

NOTHING THIS *BIG*, THOUGH.

FWOOOSH

BURNS PRETTY DIRTY, *huh?*

THAT CAN'T BE TOO HEALTHY.

YEAH, WELL. UKUR'S WORKING ON FIXING ALL THAT.

"GONNA BE *HARD* FOR A LITTLE WHILE.

"BUT THOSE KIDS ARE GONNA GROW UP *PROTECTED*.

"*STRONG*.

"*FREE*."

FOLKS UPSTAIRS BEEN HOLDING OUT ON US.

THEY'VE GOT THE TECH TO HELP US *ALL*. BUT THEY AIN'T SHARING.

UKUR'S GONNA *MAKE* 'EM SHARE.

YOU THERE! WHAT ARE YOU DOING WALLOWING IN THE MUCK?

WHOOPS.

WHOOPS?

EEP EEP

SYSTEM SAYS YOU'RE...*AKSEL*, huh?

YES, SIR.

AND YOU HAVEN'T REPORTED IN FOR A *MONTH!*

YEAH. SORRY. I GOT LOST IN THE CLIFFS...

UFF!

CRANCH

ALL RIGHT, LET'S GO.

LITTLE *TOO* NICE, I GUESS.

I'LL TELL YOU THE SAME THING I TOLD THE SENATE SUBCOMMITTEE AND THAT *AMAZON*...

...HE'S THE WORST LITTLE *WEASEL* I EVER MET.

SNUCK IN HERE PRETENDING TO BE A *REPORTER*...

"PRETENDING"?

HE GOT NOMINATED FOR A COUPLE OF *PULITZERS*, DIDN'T HE, MR. WHITE?

YOU KNOW WHAT I'M TALKING ABOUT, GORDON.

HOW'D YOU LIKE IT IF YOU FOUND OUT ONE OF YOUR COPS WAS...

...WAS *BATMAN* OR SOMETHING?

RUNNING AROUND IN A *COSTUME* FIGHTING *MANIACS?*

YOU'VE... GOT A POINT, THERE.

I *LOVED* THAT DAMN KID, YOU KNOW THAT?

BUT HE ENDANGERED THE LIVES OF EVERYONE IN THIS NEWSROOM.

IF YOU HAVE ANY OPPORTUNITY TO WORK WITH HIM...

...I STRONGLY SUGGEST YOU *DON'T*.

ALL RIGHT. CARDS ON THE TABLE.

SUPERMAN'S SHOWN UP IN GOTHAM.

FIGHTING THIS *ROBOT BATMAN,* I *KNOW*...

...AND SO DOES EVERYONE ELSE ON THE PLANET WITH INTERNET ACCESS.

MORE CARDS, GORDON.

ALL RIGHT.

HE'S... *APPROACHED* ME.

AND I'M TRYING TO FIGURE OUT WHETHER OR NOT I SHOULD *TRUST* HIM.

ALL RIGHT. CARDS ON THE TABLE.

SUPERMAN'S *CLARK KENT.*

AND CLARK WILL ALWAYS DO THE RIGHT THING.

OF COURSE, *HIS* DEFINITION OF THE RIGHT THING AND *YOURS* AND *MINE* MAY *DIFFER.*

THAT DOESN'T SOUND TOO GREAT FOR US *LITTLE PEOPLE.*

CAN'T HELP BUT NOTICE YOUR *BODYGUARD,* MS. LANE.

IS THAT THE KIND OF *TROUBLE* BEING SUPERMAN'S *FRIEND* BRINGS?

ACTUALLY, THE FACT THAT *METALLO'S* WATCHING MY BACK IS A *BONUS* I GET FOR BEING SUPERMAN'S FRIEND.

BUT YOU WOULDN'T *NEED* YOUR BACK *WATCHED* IF--

SHOULD I MAKE HIM GO AWAY, LOIS?

NO, JOHN. IT'S ALL RIGHT. JUST KEEP YOUR EYE ON EVERYONE ELSE.

I ALWAYS DO.

YEAH. MY LIFE'S... CHANGED. AND HE CAN'T JUST FIX IT.

HE'S *SUPERMAN.* NOT GOD.

SO SOMETIMES HE SCREWS IT UP. THE SAME WAY YOU AND I DO.

BUT THE ONE THING YOU CAN COUNT ON IS FOR CLARK KENT TO PUT *EVERYONE ELSE* ON THE PLANET...

AND YET HERE WE ARE.

IN *DARKNESS* AND *SMOKE* AND *SQUALOR*.

I KNOW HOW YOU SUFFER.

I KNOW YOU HAVE NOWHERE ELSE TO GO.

I KNOW YOU STILL ACHE WITH SUCH TERRIBLE HOPE.

SO HOW *DARE* I *PROMISE*?

HOW DARE I PROMISE TO YOU ONCE AGAIN THAT I WILL BRING YOU LIGHT AND WARMTH AND JOY UNDER THE WORLD, FOREVER AND EVER?

AND YET I PROMISE.

BECAUSE I KNOW WHERE THEY KEEP THEIR SUN.

RRRRRAAAAAA!

THE *ROAR* OF THE PEOPLE *SHAKES MY BONES.*

THEY *BELIEVE.*

AND GOD HELP ME...

...MAYBE *I* DO, TOO.

KENT! LISTEN TO ME!

HOW MANY SOLDIERS IN THE ARMY?

WHAT KINDS OF WEAPONS?

VULNERABILITIES?

TRANSPORTATION?

STOP.

DAMMIT, KENT! HE SAYS HE KNOWS WHERE IT IS!

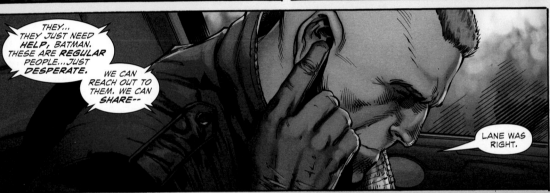

THEY... THEY JUST NEED *HELP*, BATMAN. THESE ARE *REGULAR* PEOPLE...JUST *DESPERATE*.

WE CAN REACH OUT TO THEM. WE CAN *SHARE*--

LANE WAS RIGHT.

LANE? WHAT ARE YOU TALKING ABOUT?

YOU'RE ALWAYS GOING TO DO THE RIGHT THING.

BUT YOU'VE GOT A *FUNNY IDEA* OF WHAT THAT *RIGHT THING* MIGHT BE.

BATMAN...

THAT SUBHUMAN TORE UP MY CITY.

AND HE COULD DESTROY THE WHOLE COUNTRY IF HE GOT HIS HANDS ON THAT SUN--

--AND YOU'RE SO SOFT-HEADED YOU'RE JUST ABOUT READY TO HELP HIM DO IT.

BUT IT DOESN'T MATTER.

BECAUSE UNLESS HE'S GOT A NAVY DOWN THERE, HE ISN'T GETTING IT.

SUPERMAN? HOW ARE YOU EVEN--

--THEY SAID YOU'D *LOST* YOUR *POWERS!*

WELL. THAT'S *MOSTLY* TRUE.

GOOD...

...THEN I'LL GIVE YOU A *QUICK* DEATH.

UKUR, I KNOW YOU *BLAME* ME FOR *SUBTERRANEA* LOSING ITS *POWER SOURCE*...

...BUT I'M TRYING TO *HELP* YOU.

I'VE HAD ENOUGH OF YOUR KIND OF HELP.

TODAY SUBTERRANEA HELPS *ITSELF.*

UKUR, WE'RE RUNNING OUT OF TIME.

I JOINED YOU TO GET THAT *SUN* OUT OF THE *OCEAN.*

I'M COUNTING ON YOU TO *FINISH* THAT JOB...

...WHILE *I* DEAL WITH *SUPERMAN.*

LISTEN TO ME, BOTH OF YOU! YOU CAN'T--

THEY'RE COMING!

LET'S GO, LET'S GO! PLAN B! EVERYBODY *DOWN BELOW!*

KENT, HE'S RIGHT.

TAKE THE FALL.

HE'LL JUST COME FOR YOU NEXT!

I'M BATMAN.

I CAN HANDLE IT.

LISTEN TO THAT.

NOW HE SOUNDS ALMOST LIKE YOU, BRUCE...

...BUT I'VE GOT NO IDEA WHAT'S REALLY GOING ON IN HIS HEAD.

KTHUKK

GRRRAAA!

IF IT WERE YOU IN THAT SUIT, BRUCE, I'D KNOW YOU HAD A PLAN...

NOT BAD.

I'M NOT *PLAYING*, ARTHUR! WE HAVE TO STOP *UKUR!*

KTHOOOM

KTHOOOM

KTHOOOM

...BEYOND JUST TRYING TO *BLOW* THINGS UP...

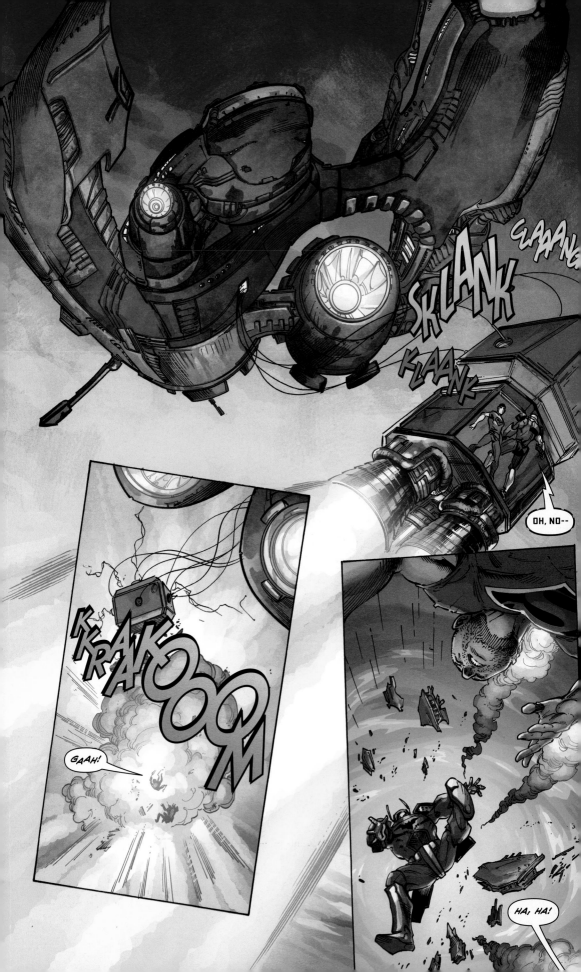

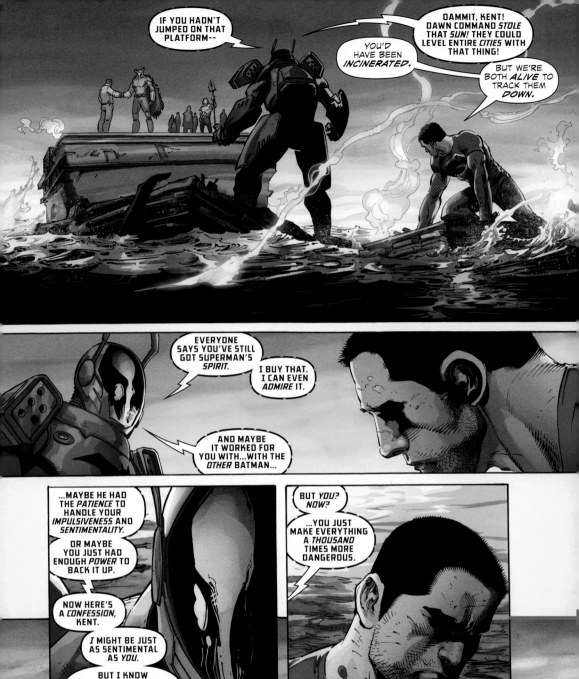

SAVAGE HUNT

GREG PAK writer **CLIFF RICHARDS** artist **BETH SOTELO** colorist **ROB LEIGH** letterer **FRANCIS MANAPUL** cover

BUT THAT *ARMORED TRUCK* LOOKS PRETTY *PROMISING.*

TRACK. SCAN.

THERE ARE THE *DAWN COMMAND BARBARIANS* I'VE BEEN TRACKING.

NO SIGN OF MY *MAIN TARGET--* THE *ARTIFICIAL SUN* THEY STOLE FROM *LUCIUS FOX'S WAYNETECH FACILITY...*

03124

BUT THEY'VE GOT THOSE *GUNS* THAT *ABSORBED* MY POWERS...

...AND THEY'VE PICKED UP A FEW MORE *ANCILLARY WEAPONS.*

REPRODUCTIONS?

NEGATIVE.

ORIGINAL.

78569

THAT *HOPLITE SWORD* HAS TO BE *THOUSANDS* OF YEARS OLD...

THAT DOESN'T MAKE ANY *SENSE.*

BUT *FINALLY...*

...I'M ABOUT TO GET SOME *ANSWERS.*

VANDAL SAVAGE, *huh?*

HA. YOU'RE STILL *QUICK* ENOUGH, AREN'T YOU?

BUT I'VE GOT *THOUSANDS* OF *YEARS* ON YOU, KENT.

THAT'S RIGHT. IMMORTAL MEGALOMANIAC. BRILLIANT, DANGEROUS...

...THIS SHOULDN'T TAKE LONG.

GRRRAAA!

SKRRRAAKKK

UNNH!

THHOOOKKK

AND THEN HE PUNCHES ME *HARD* ENOUGH TO *CRACK* TWO MOLARS.

GIVE UP. YOU'RE MARGINALLY MORE INTERESTING TO ME *ALIVE.*

IT'S IN BOTH OUR INTERESTS TO--

E'S NEVER BEEN THIS *STRONG.* AND NOW HE'S *GLOATING.*

HE'S CLEARLY PREPARED FOR THIS A LONG, *LONG* TIME.

AND NOW HE THINKS IT'LL BE A *CAKEWALK.*

GOOD.

GRRAAAA!

I ALWAYS LIKE EXCEEDING EXPECTATIONS.

LISTEN. I APPRECIATE YOU **SAVING** ME.

BUT YOU CAN'T **DO** THIS--

ACTUALLY, I THINK I ALREADY **HAVE**.

WHAT?

YOU STARTED OFF FIGHTING **BARBARIANS** WHO WERE HIJACKING MAJOR **ENERGY SOURCES**...

...AND THEN YOU FOUND OUT THEY WERE CARRYING PERFECTLY PRESERVED **WEAPONS** THAT ARE **HUNDREDS** OF YEARS OLD...

...AND THEN YOU GOT YOUR BUTT KICKED BY **VANDAL SAVAGE**...

...WHO'S SOMETHING LIKE **THREE THOUSAND** YEARS OLD.

RIGHT... SO...

SO IF WE TAP THE **A.R.G.U.S.** DATABASE OF UNUSUAL **VIRUS** ACTIVITY--

WAIT, WHAT?

OBVIOUSLY, VANDAL'S GOT A BUNCH OF WARRIORS FROM **ANCIENT TIMES** IN **SUSPENDED ANIMATION**.

OH. OBVIOUSLY...

SO WE SEARCH FOR ANY TRACES OF **ANACHRONISTIC VIRUSES** OR **BIOLOGICAL MATERIAL** AND CROSS-REF THAT FOR **MAJOR ENERGY SOURCES**...

....AND HERE WE GO.

WHOA.

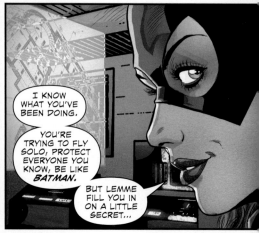

I KNOW WHAT YOU'VE BEEN DOING.

YOU'RE TRYING TO FLY SOLO, PROTECT EVERYONE YOU KNOW, BE LIKE **BATMAN**.

BUT LEMME FILL YOU IN ON A LITTLE SECRET...

carynord '15

GREG PAK writer   ARDIAN SYAF CLIFF RICHARDS pencillers VICENTE CIFUENTES CLIFF RICHARDS inkers BETH SOTELO colorist   ROB LEIGH letterer   CARY NORD cover

carynord

HURRY UP, YURI! THE BLIZZARD'S COMING!

I KNOW, DAMMIT!

BUT THE WINCH IS SHORTING OUT!

WE'RE GONNA HAVE TO HOIST IT THE REST OF THE WAY BY *HAND!*

THAT'S *CRAZY!* THAT THING WEIGHS *TWO TONS!* AND IF WE *DROP* IT, WE'RE ALL *DEAD!*

JUST SET IT *DOWN* UNTIL--

THIS IS *SUICIDE!* WE SHOULD JUST *RUN!*

AND THEN VANDAL WILL *HUNT* US *DOWN* AND *KILL* US *ALL--*

DAMMIT, ANASENKO! YOU HEARD *VANDAL SAVAGE!*

WE HAVE TO EXTRACT THAT *URANIUM,* AND WE ONLY HAVE A *WEEK!*

SKRFFRAAKK!

--INCLUDING YOUR *WIFE* AND *BOY!*

PAPA, LOOK!

OH, NO...

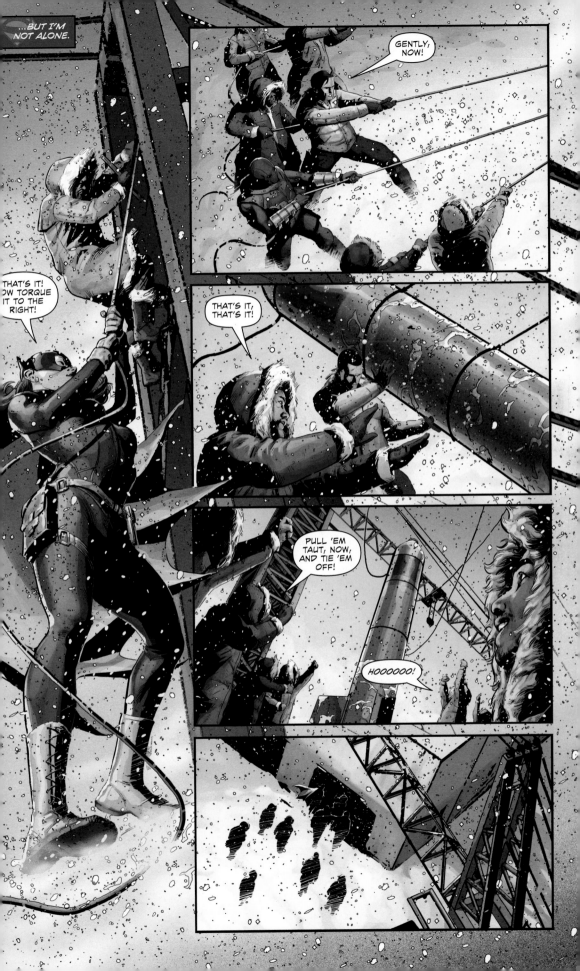

VANDAL'S STOCKPILING *ENERGY*. THIS URANIUM IS THE *LEAST* OF IT.

A BUNCH OF HIS MINIONS HAVE BEEN DRAINING MY *POWER*...

...AND HE STOLE WAYNETECH'S *ARTIFICIAL SUN*...

...WHICH COULD *INCINERATE* AN ENTIRE *CITY* BY ITSELF.

WHY'S HE MESSING AROUND *HERE* THEN?

EXACTLY. HE'S GOT TO HAVE A *BIGGER* PLAN...

...TO POWER SOMETHING... MUCH, MUCH MORE *DESTRUCTIVE*.

SOMETHING HE'S BEEN PLANNING FOR *DECADES*...

...AND THOSE SHADOW WERE *PROTECTING* IT...

EVERYONE, STAND BACK.

FTOOOM FTOOOOM

FTOOOM

WHOA...

...I STILL DON'T *TOTALLY* GET IT...

GREG PAK writer   CLIFF RICHARDS JACK HERBERT artists BETH SOTELO   WIL QUINTANA colorists   ROB LEIGH letterer   YANICK PAQUETTE   NATHAN FAIRBAIRN cover

...or if he knew that Superman had **another** friend in the shadows.

Total trust.

That's what we should aim for, right?

Pencils by Ardian Syaf for page 63